GCSE Edexcel English

Unseen Poetry

Reading poems for the first time can be a beautiful experience... unless you have to write an in-depth essay about them on the spot. Which is exactly what you'll need to do for the Unseen Poetry question in the Edexcel English Literature exams.

But don't worry. This brilliant CGP book has everything you'll need to write a top-grade answer — a big range of sample poems, plenty of practice questions, full answers and exam advice.

Once you've worked through all this, you should be able to handle any poems the examiners can throw at you!

The Poetry Guide

Published by CGP

Editors:
Izzy Bowen
Tom Carney
Andy Cashmore
Joshua James
Sean Walsh

With thanks to Rebecca Tate and Paula Barnett for the proofreading.
With thanks to Ana Pungartnik for the copyright research.

ISBN: 978 1 78294 999 2
Printed by Elanders Ltd, Newcastle upon Tyne.
Clipart from Corel®

Based on the classic CGP style created by Richard Parsons.

CONTENTS

What You Have to do in the Exam

For your Edexcel English Literature course, you'll have to sit two exams — Paper 1 and Paper 2. This book will help you prepare for the Unseen Poetry section, which is part of Paper 2.

This is how your Paper 2 exam will work

1) The Paper 2 exam lasts for 2 hours and 15 minutes. It will be split into three sections like this:

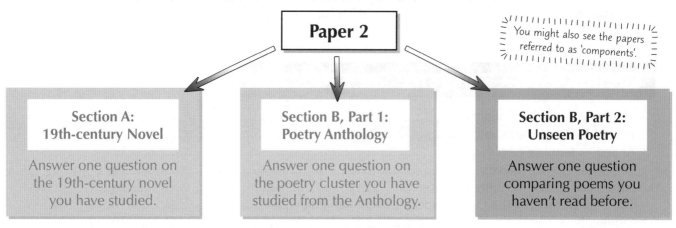

You might also see the papers referred to as 'components'.

Paper 2

Section A:
19th-century Novel

Answer one question on the 19th-century novel you have studied.

Section B, Part 1:
Poetry Anthology

Answer one question on the poetry cluster you have studied from the Anthology.

Section B, Part 2:
Unseen Poetry

Answer one question comparing poems you haven't read before.

2) For Section B, Part 2, you will be given two poems that you haven't read before and will have to answer one question about them.

3) The Unseen Poetry section is worth 20 marks — 12.5% of your entire GCSE.

4) In the exam, you should spend about 45 minutes answering the question in Section B, Part 2.

You will have to compare two unseen poems

1) To answer the question in Section B, Part 2, you'll have to compare both poems.

2) You should write about similarities and differences between the two poems. You answer should cover:

- What the poems are about — the messages, themes and ideas.
- How the poets use form, structure and language to communicate these ideas.

3) You should identify several key similarities and/or differences to write about. Every paragraph should discuss one similarity or difference between the two poems.

The examiner is looking for four main things

To impress the examiner with your answer to the question in Section B, Part 2, you need to:

1) Show that you understand what the poems are about.
2) Write about the techniques the poets use and their effect on the reader.
3) Support every point you make with quotes or examples from the poems.
4) Use the correct technical terms to describe the techniques used in the poems.

Five Steps to Analysing the Unseen Poems

When facing an unseen poem, you should follow these five steps to analyse and understand it.

1) Work out what the poem's about

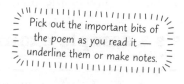
Pick out the important bits of the poem as you read it — underline them or make notes.

1) Work out the subject of the poem.
   E.g. "The poem is about the narrator coming to terms with death".

2) Look at whether it's written in the first person ("I"), second person ("you") or third person ("he / she").
   Think about who the poem is addressing — e.g. a member of the narrator's family, the reader...

2) Identify the purpose, theme or message

1) Think about what the poet is saying, why they've written the poem, or what ideas they're using.

2) The poem could be an emotional response to something. It might aim to get a response from the reader, or put across a message or an opinion about something.

3) There could be more than one purpose, theme or message in the poem.

3) Explore the emotions, moods or feelings

1) Think about the different emotions or feelings in the poem.

2) Identify the poem's mood (the general atmosphere, e.g. gloomy).

3) Look at how the poet has used different techniques to show these emotions (see step 4).

4) Identify the techniques used in the poem

1) Pick out the different techniques the poet has used and how they create the emotions, moods or feelings in the poem. Make sure you use the correct technical terms when you write about these techniques:

   - Form and structure — the type of poem, e.g. a sonnet, and the order and arrangement of ideas in the poem. Also look at rhyme and rhythm, changes in the lengths of lines or stanzas, and any changes in mood or theme.
   - Poetic devices — things like metaphors, alliteration, personification and enjambment.
   - Imagery — language that creates a picture in your mind, including things like metaphors and similes.

2) Think about why the poet has used these techniques, and what effects they create.

5) Include your thoughts and feelings about the poem

1) Examiners love to hear what you think of a poem and how it makes you feel.

2) Think about how well the poem gets its message across and what impact it had on you.

3) Try not to use "I" though. Don't say "I feel sad about the end of the narrator's relationship" — it's much better to say "It invites the reader to share in the narrator's sense of sadness at the end of the relationship."

4) Think about any other ways that the poem could be interpreted.

EXAM TIP

Always support your arguments with quotes and examples...

Back up every point you make with evidence from the poems, otherwise you'll miss out on easy marks.
As you're analysing the poems, underline a few key quotes that you could use to support your arguments.

Sample Exam Question

The question in Section B, Part 2 will ask you to <u>compare</u> the unseen poems. <u>Read</u> the question carefully and underline the <u>key words</u>, then <u>annotate</u> the poems to pick out the important bits. Here's an example...

Here's a sample exam question

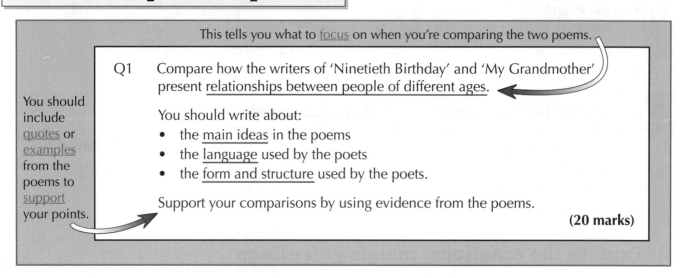

This tells you what to <u>focus</u> on when you're comparing the two poems.

Q1   Compare how the writers of 'Ninetieth Birthday' and 'My Grandmother' present <u>relationships between people of different ages</u>.

You should write about:
• the <u>main ideas</u> in the poems
• the <u>language</u> used by the poets
• the <u>form and structure</u> used by the poets.

Support your comparisons by using evidence from the poems.

(20 marks)

You should include <u>quotes</u> or <u>examples</u> from the poems to <u>support</u> your points.

This is how you might annotate the first poem

<u>Read</u> through the poem, and <u>jot down</u> your ideas about bits that <u>stand out</u>.

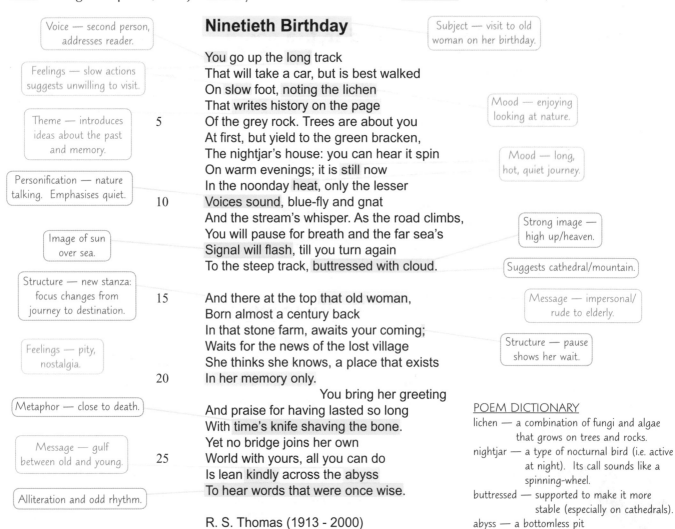

Voice — second person, addresses reader.

Subject — visit to old woman on her birthday.

Ninetieth Birthday

Feelings — slow actions suggests unwilling to visit.

Theme — introduces ideas about the past and memory.

Personification — nature talking. Emphasises quiet.

Image of sun over sea.

Structure — new stanza: focus changes from journey to destination.

Feelings — pity, nostalgia.

Metaphor — close to death.

Message — gulf between old and young.

Alliteration and odd rhythm.

Mood — enjoying looking at nature.

Mood — long, hot, quiet journey.

Strong image — high up/heaven.

Suggests cathedral/mountain.

Message — impersonal/ rude to elderly.

Structure — pause shows her wait.

You go up the long track
That will take a car, but is best walked
On slow foot, noting the lichen
That writes history on the page
Of the grey rock. Trees are about you
At first, but yield to the green bracken,
The nightjar's house: you can hear it spin
On warm evenings; it is still now
In the noonday heat, only the lesser
Voices sound, blue-fly and gnat
And the stream's whisper. As the road climbs,
You will pause for breath and the far sea's
Signal will flash, till you turn again
To the steep track, buttressed with cloud.

And there at the top that old woman,
Born almost a century back
In that stone farm, awaits your coming;
Waits for the news of the lost village
She thinks she knows, a place that exists
In her memory only.
                    You bring her greeting
And praise for having lasted so long
With time's knife shaving the bone.
Yet no bridge joins her own
World with yours, all you can do
Is lean kindly across the abyss
To hear words that were once wise.

R. S. Thomas (1913 - 2000)

5
10
15
20
25

POEM DICTIONARY
lichen — a combination of fungi and algae that grows on trees and rocks.
nightjar — a type of nocturnal bird (i.e. active at night). Its call sounds like a spinning-wheel.
buttressed — supported to make it more stable (especially on cathedrals).
abyss — a bottomless pit

Section One — Exam Advice

Sample Exam Question

This is how you might annotate the second poem

<u>Read</u> the poem and <u>mark</u> the key bits. Use the <u>bullet points</u> in the question to guide you on what to look for.

Poem has four stanzas of six lines each. More structured than 'Ninetieth Birthday'.

Iambic pentameter used throughout.

Alliteration.

Voice — first person, describes personal memories. Contrasts with more distant relationship in 'Ninetieth Birthday'.

Enjambment.

Metaphor — shows isolation.

Theme — obsession with material things.

Image linked to death.

My Grandmother

She kept an antique shop – or it kept her.
Among Apostle spoons and Bristol glass,
The faded silks, the heavy furniture,
She watched her own reflection in the brass
5   Salvers and silver bowls, as if to prove
Polish was all, there was no need of love.

And I remember how I once refused
To go out with her, since I was afraid.
It was perhaps a wish not to be used
10   Like antique objects. Though she never said
That she was hurt, I still could feel the guilt
Of that refusal, guessing how she felt.

Later, too frail to keep a shop, she put
All her best things in one narrow room.
15   The place smelt old, of things too long kept shut,
The smell of absences where shadows come
That can't be polished. There was nothing then
To give her own reflection back again.

And when she died I felt no grief at all,
20   Only the guilt of what I once refused.
I walked into her room among the tall
Sideboards and cupboards – things she never used
But needed; and no finger marks were there,
Only the new dust falling through the air.

Elizabeth Jennings

Subject — the narrator's relationship with their grandmother.

Theme — cold relationship.

Theme — treating people like objects.

Feelings — narrator's guilt.

Feelings — loneliness. Similar to 'Ninetieth Birthday'.

Theme — isolation. Same as in 'Ninetieth Birthday'.

Regular rhyme, ABABCC throughout. All full rhymes in final stanza.

POEM DICTIONARY
Salver — a flat tray

Spend five minutes planning your answer

1) Always <u>plan</u> your answer <u>before</u> you start — that way, you're less likely to forget something <u>important</u>. Here's how to do it:

- Focus on <u>several key points</u> from each poem.
- Remember to write about <u>what</u> the poet says and <u>how</u> they say it.
- Make sure that <u>each</u> one of your points is <u>comparing</u> something between the poems.
- Include a few <u>quotes</u> or <u>examples</u> so you remember to <u>use</u> them in your answer.
- <u>Don't</u> spend <u>too long</u> on your plan. It's only <u>rough work</u>, so you don't need to use full sentences.

2) Now you know all about planning, turn over the page for an <u>example plan</u> and <u>worked answer</u> to the sample exam question...

Worked Answer

Once you've understood the question and annotated both poems, you'll be ready to plan your answer. Oh, and then you've got to write your answer, too...

This is how you could plan your answer

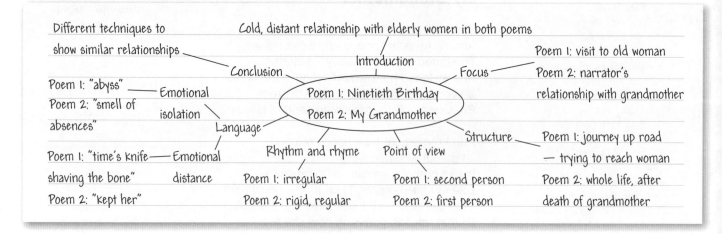

Different techniques to show similar relationships

Poem 1: "abyss"
Poem 2: "smell of absences" — Emotional isolation

Poem 1: "time's knife shaving the bone" — Emotional distance
Poem 2: "kept her"

Conclusion

Cold, distant relationship with elderly women in both poems

Introduction

Poem 1: Ninetieth Birthday
Poem 2: My Grandmother

Language

Rhythm and rhyme
Poem 1: irregular
Poem 2: rigid, regular

Point of view
Poem 1: second person
Poem 2: first person

Focus

Poem 1: visit to old woman
Poem 2: narrator's relationship with grandmother

Structure

Poem 1: journey up road — trying to reach woman
Poem 2: whole life, after death of grandmother

This is how you could answer the sample exam question

Show that you've understood the question.

'Ninetieth Birthday' and 'My Grandmother' both present rather distant relationships between two people of different ages. The poets use narrative voice, form, structure and language in contrasting ways to present these relationships.

Consider what the two poems are about and their main ideas.

The two poems focus on different aspects of relationships between younger and older people. 'My Grandmother' is about a specific, personal relationship between the narrator and their grandmother, and the narrator's feelings of guilt after her death.

Phrases like 'in contrast' can be used to show a difference.

'Ninetieth Birthday', in contrast, explores the relationships between younger and older people more generally through a description of a visit to an elderly woman. Here we know far less about the characters, although the reference to "that stone farm" suggests the visitor knows the woman's home well and may be related to her. This lack of information helps turn the poem into a general comment on relationships between young and old.

Compare the structure of the poems.

The two poems are structured differently to express the poets' ideas. 'Ninetieth Birthday' follows the visitor on a physical journey up a road to the old woman's home. This suggests the visitor is trying to reach the old woman, both physically and emotionally. 'My Grandmother', in contrast, has a structure that follows the narrator's life, starting with their childhood and ending with their grandmother's death. This gives the reader a clear sense of the pair's relationship, and suggests that the narrator is contemplating the grandmother after her death and trying to understand how they feel about her.

Think about the mood and feelings in the each poem.

Explain how the techniques in the poems affect the reader.

The different points of view of the two poems reflect their different focuses. 'Ninetieth Birthday' is written in the second person. By addressing the reader directly, Thomas encourages the reader to think about their own relationships with the elderly. In contrast, 'My Grandmother' uses the first person to present the poem as a reflection on the narrator's relationship with their own grandmother. This gives 'My Grandmother' a more personal tone than 'Ninetieth Birthday'.

Remember to compare the two poems throughout your answer.

Worked Answer

The way each poem is organised reflects the relationships between younger and older people in the poems. 'My Grandmother' has four regular stanzas of six lines each, and a regular rhyme scheme, ABABCC. This regularity gives the poem a controlled, almost rigid tone, which may reflect the rigid, cold relationship between the narrator and their grandmother. In contrast, 'Ninetieth Birthday' has no regular rhyme scheme. The poet uses a lot of enjambment, for example "you can hear it spin / On warm evenings", and there are several caesurae, such as the full stop in line 5. These techniques create an irregular rhythm with lots of pauses, forcing the reader to stop briefly as they read, reflecting how, in the first stanza, the visitor stops repeatedly on their journey to "that stone farm" because they are reluctant to spend time with the old woman.

In both poems, the language used demonstrates a sense of emotional distance between a younger and an older person. The metaphor "time's knife shaving the bone" in 'Ninetieth Birthday' represents how close the woman is to death; its shocking nature emphasises this idea vividly. It may also reflect the physical effects of ageing on the body. The violence of this metaphor contrasts with the visitor's more friendly "greeting" and "praise", suggesting they don't understand the struggles of old age that the woman is going through. 'My Grandmother' similarly uses language to express emotional distance. In the first stanza, the narrator describes the grandmother as an antique, saying that the antique shop "kept her". This phrase implies that she is an object and that the narrator may not be thinking of her needs as a person. This again reflects their cold personal relationship, and, as in 'Ninetieth Birthday', it also hints at the difficulty younger people may have in understanding and relating to older people.

This distance is emphasised by the metaphorical language used in both poems to describe the women's emotional isolation. In Jennings' poem, the grandmother is surrounded by "The smell of absences", a metaphor which shows that the grandmother's focus on her possessions, rather than "love", has left her emotionally isolated. Even though she has "All her best things" around her, she has no close relationships — "absences" surround her, rather than people. Similarly, in 'Ninetieth Birthday', Thomas uses metaphorical language to show that the old woman is emotionally cut off. The metaphor of "the abyss" vividly describes the way the woman is separated from others, suggesting that the visitor finds it impossible to reach her in "her own / World". These descriptions of isolation encourage the reader to feel pity for the older women, by suggesting their real feelings and implying they may be unhappy being alone.

Although the focus, form, structure and language used in 'Ninetieth Birthday' and 'My Grandmother' are different, both poems use these techniques to present similarly distant relationships between people of different ages. In this way, both poems explore the issue of how younger and older people can relate to each other.

Comment on changes in the rhythm and the effect they have.

Introduce your paragraphs with a comparison.

Use quotes to support your argument.

Show that you understand the imagery in the poems.

Write about how form conveys meaning.

Use technical terms where appropriate.

Show your own personal response to the poems.

Summarise the similarities and differences in your conclusion.

Think about how to organise your time...

There's lots to do in Section B, Part 2, so you need to watch the clock. Make sure you give yourself enough time for each bit: reading the poems, planning your answer and then writing it. The trick is to practice...

Handbag

This section gives you loads of <u>poems</u> and some rather tasty <u>questions</u> about them. <u>Read</u> each poem, <u>annotate</u> it, then have a go at the <u>questions</u>. They're great practice for your Unseen Poetry exam.

Ruth Fainlight was born in New York in 1931, but moved to England when she was fifteen. She's published <u>short stories</u> and <u>poems</u>, including this one about her mum's old handbag.

Handbag

My mother's old leather handbag,
crowded with letters she carried
all through the war. The smell
of my mother's handbag: mints
5   and lipstick and Coty powder.
The look of those letters, softened
and worn at the edges, opened,
read, and refolded so often.
Letters from my father. Odour
10   of leather and powder, which ever
since then has meant womanliness,
and love, and anguish, and war.

Ruth Fainlight

<u>POEM DICTIONARY</u>
Coty powder — a face powder

Carrying letters round in
your bag can get messy.

Ruth Fainlight

I know by now you'll be desperate to show off your <u>poetry analysis skills</u>, so here's your chance...
<u>Read</u> and <u>annotate</u> the poem on p.8, then have a go at answering these <u>questions</u>.

Warm-up Questions

Q1   Explain briefly what you think the poem is about.

Q2   Why do you think the narrator is looking through their mother's bag now?

Q3   Briefly describe the emotions that the poet puts across.
     How does the poet show these emotions?

Q4   What does the phrase "crowded with letters" suggest about the narrator's mother?

Q5   Why do you think the poet uses enjambment to break up the phrase "carried / all through the war"?

Q6   How does the poet convey the way the handbag smells? Why do you think these smells are important to the narrator?

Q7   Why do you think the narrator specifies the brand of powder ("Coty") used by their mother?
     What effect does this have?

Q8   How does the poet use the sense of touch in this poem?

Q9   Why do you think "Letters from my father." is the only complete sentence written on a single line?

Q10 The poet repeats the word "and" three times in the final line.
     What effect does this have?

Q11 Why do you think the poet chose not to use a rhyme scheme in the poem?
     Explain your answer.

Jumper

Tony Harrison was born in Leeds in 1937. He has written <u>plays</u> and <u>poetry</u>, as well as <u>translating</u> works from ancient Greek and French. This poem was published in the <u>1970s</u>, but part of it is a memory from <u>World War Two</u>. During the war, people hid in bomb shelters for <u>protection</u> during bombing raids.

Jumper

When I want some sort of human metronome
to beat calm celebration out of fear
like that when German bombs fell round our home
it's my mother's needles, knitting, that I hear,
5   the click of needles steady though walls shake.
The stitches, plain or purl, were never dropped.
Bombs fell all that night until daybreak
but, not for a moment, did the knitting stop.
Though we shivered in the cellar-shelter's cold
10   and the whistling bombs sent shivers through the walls
I know now why she made her scared child hold
the skeins she wound so calmly into balls.

We open presents wrapped before she died.
With that same composure shown in that attack
15   she'd known the time to lay her wools aside —

the jumper I open's shop-bought, and is black!

Tony Harrison

<u>POEM DICTIONARY</u>
metronome — a machine that ticks at a constant speed to help musicians stay in time
plain and purl — types of stitch in knitting
skein — a length of wool that has been loosely twisted or coiled

Tony Harrison

In the exam you'll have to read not one but <u>two poems</u> that you haven't seen before, and then <u>compare</u> them. Have a go at these <u>questions</u> to help you get to grips with 'Jumper', then try the exam-style question.

Warm-up Questions

Q1   Explain briefly what you think the poem is about.

Q2   How does the poet suggest that the narrator and their mother were in danger during the bombing?

Q3   Why do you think the narrator's mother made them hold the wool as she was knitting?

Q4   Briefly describe the emotions that the poet puts across. How does the poet show these emotions?

Q5   The poet uses the words "shivered" and "shivers" on consecutive lines. What effect does this have?

Q6   a) How are the last four lines of the poem different from the first twelve lines?

    b) Why do you think the poet has done this?

Q7   How does the poet use the senses in the poem? Do you think this is effective?

Q8   Find an example of onomatopoeia in the poem and explain its effect.

Q9   What do you notice about the rhythm of the poem? What effect does this have?

Q10   Why do you think it is significant that the jumper is "shop-bought" and "black"? Why has this description been separated from the rest of the stanza?

Exam-style Question

Compare how the narrators' memories of their mothers are presented in 'Handbag' and 'Jumper'. You should think about:
- the main ideas in the poems
- the form, structure and language used by the poets.

Section Two — Unseen Poetry Practice

At Sea

Jennifer Copley was born in Cumbria and, after living in Oxford and London, returned to make the area her home. She has published several collections of poetry and was made South Cumbria Poet Laureate in 2005.

At Sea

With nothing to do now he's gone,
she dusts the house,
sweeps the bleached verandah clear of sand.
The broom leaves a trail of grit on the step,
5   a sprinkling under the hook where it hangs.

A coat for a pillow,
she sleeps downstairs,
dreams the loathed ocean is coming for her,
climbing the cliffs,
10   creeping in through the door.

She wakes to the screaming gulls,
his shirts on the line
and the high tide's breakers'
chill in her arms.

Jennifer Copley

POEM DICTIONARY
verandah — an outdoor part of a house that usually
        runs along the front of the building.
breakers — waves

John and Adrian had found
a much more interesting
use for their brooms.

Jennifer Copley

Once you've <u>annotated</u> 'At Sea', try these <u>warm-up questions</u> to help you get to grips with it. When you feel you know it <u>inside out</u>, turn over the page and get to know the poem you'll be <u>comparing</u> it to.

Warm-up Questions

Q1   Briefly explain what you think the poem is about.

Q2   What impressions do you get of the woman's feelings in the first stanza?
How does the poet portray these feelings?

Q3   Find an example of sibilance in the poem.
Describe the effect it has.

Q4   Why do you think the woman uses a "coat for a pillow"?

Q5   Why does the poet describe the ocean as "loathed"?

Q6   Find an example of personification in the poem and explain its effect.

Q7   What is the effect of the poet's use of sound in the final stanza?

Q8   Do you think the woman's feelings have changed by the end of the poem?
Explain your answer.

Q9   What do you notice about the poem's rhythm and rhyme scheme?
How does this reflect the woman's feelings and behaviour?

Q10   How does the structure of the poem reflect the woman's experience while waiting at home for the man to return?

Q11   Why do you think the poem is called 'At Sea'? What does this title tell you about the woman and the absent man?

The Sea

James Reeves was born in 1909 near London and died in 1978. As well as poetry, he wrote stories for both children and adults. This poem is all about the sea and its changing behaviour.

The Sea

The sea is a hungry dog,
Giant and grey.
He rolls on the beach all day.
With his clashing teeth and shaggy jaws
5   Hour upon hour he gnaws
The rumbling, tumbling stones,
And 'Bones, bones, bones, bones!'
The giant sea-dog moans,
Licking his greasy paws.

10   And when the night wind roars
And the moon rocks in the stormy cloud,
He bounds to his feet and snuffs and sniffs,
Shaking his wet sides over the cliffs,
And howls and hollos long and loud.

15   But on quiet days in May or June,
When even the grasses on the dune
Play no more their reedy tune,
With his head between his paws
He lies on the sandy shores,
20   So quiet, so quiet, he scarcely snores.

James Reeves

James Reeves

Here's another set of <u>questions</u> for your delight and delectation. Remember to keep flicking back to 'At Sea' on p.12 as you answer the <u>exam-style question</u> to make sure you haven't missed anything.

Warm-up Questions

Q1   In just one sentence, explain what you think the poem is about.

Q2   a) What impact does the extended metaphor of the dog have on the way the sea is presented?

       b) How effective do you think this is?

Q3   What is really happening when the dog "gnaws" on the "rumbling, tumbling stones"?

Q4   What is the purpose of the repetition in line 7?

Q5   What is the effect of alliteration in the second stanza?

Q6   How does the mood change over the course of the poem?

Q7   How is sibilance used in the poem?
       What is its effect?

Q8   What do you notice about the use of rhyme in the poem?
       What effect does this have?

Q9   What overall impression do you think the poet is trying to give of the sea?
       Explain your answer.

Exam-style Question

Compare how the sea is presented in 'At Sea' and 'The Sea'. You should think about:
- the main ideas in the poems
- the form, structure and language used by the poets.

Horse Whisperer

Andrew Forster was born in South Yorkshire in 1964. This poem about a horse whisperer comes from his collection _Fear of Thunder_, which was shortlisted for the 2008 Forward Prize for Best First Collection.

Horse Whisperer

They shouted for me
when their horses snorted, when restless
hooves traced circles in the earth
and shimmering muscles refused the plough.
5   My secret was a spongy tissue, pulled bloody
from the mouth of a just-born foal,
scented with rosemary, cinnamon,
a charm to draw the tender giants
to my hands.

10   They shouted for me
when their horses reared at burning straw
and eyes revolved in stately heads.
I would pull a frog's wishbone,
tainted by meat, from a pouch,
15   a new fear to fight the fear of fire,
so I could lead the horses,
like helpless children, to safety.

I swore I would protect
this legacy of whispers
20   but the tractor came over the fields
like a warning. I was the life-blood
no longer. From pulpits
I was scorned as demon and witch.
Pitchforks drove me from villages and farms.

25   My gifts were the tools of revenge.
A foul hex above a stable door
so a trusted stallion could be ridden
no more. Then I joined the stampede,
with others of my kind,
30   To countries far from our trade.

Still I miss them. Shire, Clydesdale, Suffolk.
The searing breath, glistening veins,
steady tread and the pride,
most of all the pride.

The term 'horse whisperer' was used to describe people who would tame unruly horses using their voice. Owing to the secrecy of the trade, many people believed horse whisperers used a form of witchcraft.

Andrew Forster

POEM DICTIONARY
hex — curse, evil spell
Shire, Clydesdale, Suffolk — breeds of horses

Andrew Forster

Woah, woah, hold your horses — there are a few obstacles you should jump over before moving on to the next page. Here are some practice equestrians to test your skills — wait no, they're practice questions...

Warm-up Questions

Q1   Briefly summarise what you think the poem is about.

Q2   Who do you think the narrator is referring to as "They" in the first line?

Q3   What is the effect of starting the first two stanzas with the line "They shouted for me"?

Q4   Give an example of a simile used in the poem.
       What effect does it create?

Q5   How does the poem change in the third stanza?

Q6   Give an example from the poem to explain how magical language is used to create:

       a) a positive atmosphere   b) a negative atmosphere

Q7   How does the poet present the narrator's feelings about machinery?

Q8   Why do you think the poet uses enjambment in the phrase
       "so a trusted stallion could be ridden / no more."?

Q9   What is suggested by the phrase "I joined the stampede"?
       What effect does this have?

Q10   a) Explain how the tense that the poem is in changes in the final stanza.

       b) What is the effect of each of the tenses used in the poem?

Q11   Do you think the narrator loses their sense of control as the poem progresses?
       How does the poet give this impression?

The Bereavement of the Lion-Keeper

Sheenagh Pugh is a British <u>poet</u>, and has also published <u>novels</u> and <u>translations</u>. She lives in Shetland, and lots of her poems feature northern European landscapes. Not this one though — this one's about lions...

The Bereavement of the Lion-Keeper

for Sheraq Omar

Who stayed, long after his pay stopped,
in the zoo with no visitors,
just keepers and captives, moth-eaten,
growing old together.

5   Who begged for meat in the market-place
as times grew hungrier,
and cut it up small to feed him,
since his teeth were gone.

Who could stroke his head, who knew
10   how it felt to plunge fingers
into rough glowing fur, who has heard
the deepest purr in the world.

Who curled close to him, wrapped in his warmth,
his pungent scent, as the bombs fell,
15   who has seen him asleep so often,
but never like this.

Who knew that elderly lions
were not immortal, that it was bound
to happen, that he died peacefully,
20   in the course of nature,

but who knows no way to let go
of love, to walk out of sunlight,
to be an old man in a city
without a lion.

Sheenagh Pugh

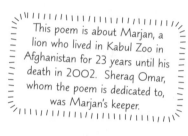

This poem is about Marjan, a lion who lived in Kabul Zoo in Afghanistan for 23 years until his death in 2002. Sheraq Omar, whom the poem is dedicated to, was Marjan's keeper.

Try as he might, Felix's purring never seemed to impress anyone.

Sheenagh Pugh

Sob Such a sad poem. I'm going in search of cake and ice cream to cheer myself up. You, however, need to <u>read</u> and <u>annotate</u> the poem and try these <u>questions</u> before you indulge in any sugary treats. Sorry.

Warm-up Questions

Q1   Briefly describe what you think the poem is about.

Q2   How does the poet suggest that the keeper was devoted to the lion and his job?

Q3   What do you think the line "wrapped in his warmth, / his pungent scent, as the bombs fell," suggests?

Q4   How does the poet appeal to different senses? Give some examples and explain their effect.

Q5   a) In what way does the poem show similarities between the ageing lion and the keeper?

         b) How does that make the reader feel?

Q6   Briefly describe the emotions that the poem puts across.

Q7   Do you think there is a feeling of hope in the poem? Pick out some quotes to explain your view.

Q8   Each stanza apart from the last one starts with the word "Who...". What is the effect of this?

Q9   Which of the six stanzas do you find the most effective in showing the keeper's emotions? Explain your answer.

Exam-style Question

Compare how relationships between humans and animals are presented in 'Horse Whisperer' and 'The Bereavement of the Lion-Keeper'. You should think about:
- the main ideas in the poems
- the form, structure and language used by the poets.

Originally

Carol Ann Duffy was born in Glasgow in 1955. She was the first woman and first Scottish person to be named Poet Laureate. Her poem, 'Originally', describes her childhood experience of moving to England.

Originally

We came from our own country in a red room
which fell through the fields, our mother singing
our father's name to the turn of the wheels.
My brothers cried, one of them bawling, *Home,*
5   *Home,* as the miles rushed back to the city,
the street, the house, the vacant rooms
where we didn't live any more. I stared
at the eyes of a blind toy, holding its paw.

All childhood is an emigration. Some are slow,
10   leaving you standing, resigned, up an avenue
where no one you know stays. Others are sudden.
Your accent wrong. Corners, which seem familiar,
leading to unimagined pebble-dashed estates, big boys
eating worms and shouting words you don't understand.
15   My parents' anxiety stirred like a loose tooth
in my head. *I want our own country*, I said.

But then you forget, or don't recall, or change,
and, seeing your brother swallow a slug, feel only
a skelf of shame. I remember my tongue
20   shedding its skin like a snake, my voice
in the classroom sounding just like the rest. Do I only think
I lost a river, culture, speech, sense of first space
and the right place? Now, *Where do you come from?*
strangers ask. *Originally?* And I hesitate.

Carol Ann Duffy

POEM DICTIONARY
skelf — Scottish dialect word that means a splinter or small piece of wood.

Carol Ann Duffy

Originally, we wanted a page of cute dog photos here, but these <u>practice questions</u> will be more useful.
Make <u>notes</u> around the poem as you go — this will help you do the <u>exam-style question</u> over the page...

Warm-up Questions

Q1   Briefly explain what you think the poem is about.

Q2   How do you think the narrator feels in the first stanza?
      How does the poet give this impression?

Q3   What is the effect of the repetition of "Home" in the first stanza?

Q4   The narrator shifts from using "we" to "I" in the first stanza.
      What effect does this have?

Q5   What is suggested by the metaphor "All childhood is an emigration."?

Q6   How does the poet create a feeling of confusion in the second stanza?

Q7   In the poem, the narrator sees some boys "eating worms" and her brother "swallow a slug".
      How does the way these events are presented show her changing attitude to her new home?

Q8   Why do you think the poet chose to use a Scottish dialect word, "skelf", in line 19?

Q9   Identify one simile in the poem. Why do you think the poet has used it?

Q10   What is the effect of the poet's use of direct speech in the poem?

Q11   What do you notice about the use of rhyme in the poem?
      How does this reflect the events in the poem?

Q12   Do you think the narrator is sure of her identity by the end of the poem?
      Explain your answer.

Hard Water

Jean Sprackland was born in Burton upon Trent, in the Midlands, in 1962. 'Hard Water', published in 2003, was inspired by Burton — a town famous for its breweries, which use the local hard water to brew the beer.

Hard Water

I tried the soft stuff on holiday in Wales,
a mania of teadrinking and hairwashing,
excitable soap which never rinsed away,

but I loved coming home to this.
5   Flat. Straight. Like the vowels,
like the straight talk: *hey up me duck*.
I'd run the tap with its swimming-pool smell,
get it cold and anaesthetic. Stand the glass
and let the little fizz of anxiety settle.
10   Honest water, bright and not quite clean.
The frankness of limestone, of gypsum,
the sour steam of cooling towers,
the alchemical taste of brewing.

On pitiless nights, I had to go for the bus
15   before last orders. I'd turn up my face,
let rain scald my eyelids and lips.
It couldn't lie. Fell thick
with a payload of acid. No salt –
this rain had forgotten the sea.
20   I opened my mouth, speaking nothing
in spite of my book-learning.
I let a different cleverness wash my tongue.
It tasted of work, the true taste
of early mornings, the blunt taste
25   of *don't get mardy*, of *too bloody deep for me*,
fierce lovely water that marked me for life
as belonging, regardless.

Jean Sprackland

POEM DICTIONARY
hard water — water containing lots of minerals
gypsum — a type of mineral
alchemical — being related to alchemy (the medieval science of changing
        things that aren't worth anything into something valuable).
payload — the cargo carried by a vehicle
mardy — dialect word for grumpy or sulky

'What do you want?'

Section Two — Unseen Poetry Practice

Jean Sprackland

A few warm-up questions should help turn this hard water into soft water. Then have a go at the exam-style question below — keep flicking back to 'Originally' on page 20 to make sure you haven't missed anything.

Warm-up Questions

Q1   Explain what the poem is about in a sentence or two.

Q2   What effect does the use of a first-person narrator have in the poem?

Q3   Describe the form of the poem. What effect does it have?

Q4   How does the tone of the poem change at the start of the second stanza?

Q5   What is the effect of the line "Flat. Straight. Like the vowels," (line 5)?

Q6   What technique does the poet use to compare the hard water to the local people?

Q7   Find an example of sibilance in the poem and explain the effect it has.

Q8   What does the narrator mean by "a different cleverness" in line 22?

Q9   What evidence is there in the poem to suggest that the narrator is proud of where they come from?

Q10   a) Give one example of dialect that is used in the poem.

       b) Why might this dialect have been used?

Exam-style Question

Compare how feelings towards particular places are presented in 'Originally' and 'Hard Water'. You should think about:
- the main ideas in the poems
- the form, structure and language used by the poets.

Tattoos

Brian Patten was born in Liverpool in 1946. He became well known in the 1960s for his efforts to make poetry <u>accessible</u> to wider audiences. Many of his poems have been <u>translated</u> into various other languages.

Tattoos

No doubt in her youth
The many tattoos on my grandmother's arms
Were bold and clear:
No grave-marks or burst blood vessels sullied
5   the breast of the blue-bird that flew
        upwards from her wrist-bone;
On her biceps
The sails on the three-decked galleon were not yellow or
      wrinkled,
10   And each angry thorn on the blue-stemmed rose was
      needle-sharp,
Its folded petals unblurred by time.
A child, I studied those tattoos intently —
Back then they seemed as mysterious as runes to me.
15   But all those tribal decorations went the way of her own
      bravado.
Ageing, the colours faded,
And her world shrank to a small island in the brain,
A tumour on which memory was shipwrecked
20   Till finally that galleon came to rest
One fathom down beneath Liverpool clay,
Its sails deflated, the blue-bird mute,
The rose gone to seed.

Brian Patten

<u>POEM DICTIONARY</u>
sullied — spoiled the quality of
galleon — a large sailing ship
runes — can mean either the letters of ancient alphabets, or small, magical rocks / pieces of bone.
one fathom — a unit of length measuring 6 feet (usually used for water depth).

Brian Patten

Read and annotate the poem on page 24, then answer these practice questions. They'll help you get to know the poem inside out. After you've done that, feel free to give yourself a Patten the back...

Warm-up Questions

Q1   Briefly explain what you think the poem is about.

Q2   What is the effect of the poem being written from the grandchild's point of view rather than from the point of view of the grandmother?

Q3   Briefly describe the emotions that the poet puts across.
      How does the poet show these emotions?

Q4   What do the grandmother's fading tattoos represent?

Q5   Why do you think the poet included language associated with sailing?

Q6   What does the word "bravado" suggest about the grandmother's character?

Q7   Describe how you think the narrator's feelings towards their grandmother changed as they grew older.

Q8   Briefly describe the structure of the poem.
      What effect does this structure have?

Q9   Why do you think the poet says that the grandmother's world "shrank to a small island in the brain"?

Q10   What does the metaphor "memory was shipwrecked" suggest about the narrator's grandmother?

Q11   What idea do you think the poet is trying to convey by having the galleon end up "One fathom down beneath Liverpool clay"?

The Ageing Schoolmaster

Vernon Scannell was born in Spilsby, Lincolnshire in 1922. He served in the army during the Second World War before becoming a teacher in the 1950s. His poems often centre around the theme of mortality.

The Ageing Schoolmaster

And now another autumn morning finds me
With chalk dust on my sleeve and in my breath,
Preoccupied with vague, habitual speculation
On the huge inevitability of death.

5   Not wholly wretched, yet knowing absolutely
That I shall never reacquaint myself with joy,
I sniff the smell of ink and chalk and my mortality
And think of when I rolled, a gormless boy,

And rollicked round the playground of my hours,
10   And wonder when precisely tolled the bell
Which summoned me from summer liberties
And brought me to this chill autumnal cell

From which I gaze upon the april faces
That gleam before me, like apples ranged on shelves,
15   And yet I feel no pinch or prick of envy
Nor would I have them know their sentenced selves.

With careful effort I can separate the faces,
The dull, the clever, the various shapes and sizes,
But in the autumn shades I find I only
20   Brood upon death, who carries off all the prizes.

Vernon Scannell

Even the pupils found the prospect
of double chemistry *unappeeling*.

Vernon Scannell

This is the <u>second poem</u> in the pair. Soon, it will be time to <u>compare</u> it with the first poem, just like you will in the exam. Before you start comparing them though, <u>familiarise</u> yourself with these <u>warm-up questions</u>.

Warm-up Questions

Q1   Explain what the poem is about in a sentence or two.

Q2   What does the first line "And now another autumn morning finds me" suggest about the narrator?

Q3   How would you describe the mood in the second stanza? How does the poet create this mood?

Q4   Do you think the narrator would like to be a "boy" again? Explain your answer.

Q5   Read the second stanza. Find an example of where the poet uses language that appeals to the senses and explain its effect.

Q6   What could Scannell be referring to when he writes "this chill autumnal cell" in line 12?

Q7   Give one example of a simile used in the poem. What effect does it have?

Q8   What do you think the poet is trying to say about:
a) youth   b) getting older   c) death

Q9   What is significant about the use of seasons in the poem?

Q10   Identify one example of personification in the poem. What effect does it have on the reader?

Exam-style Question

Compare how ageing is presented in 'Tattoos' and 'The Ageing Schoolmaster'.
You should think about:

- the main ideas in the poems
- the form, structure and language used by the poets.

Island Man

Grace Nichols was born in Guyana in 1950. She was a teacher and journalist in the Caribbean until she moved to Britain in 1977. Both British and Caribbean cultures and how they interlink are important to her.

Island Man

(for a Caribbean island man in London who still wakes up to the sound of the sea)

Morning
and island man wakes up
to the sound of blue surf
in his head
5   the steady breaking and wombing

wild seabirds
and fishermen pushing out to sea
the sun surfacing defiantly

from the east
10   of his small emerald island
he always comes back   groggily groggily

Comes back to sands
of a grey metallic soar
                to surge of wheels
15   to dull North Circular roar

muffling muffling
his crumpled pillow waves
island man heaves himself

Another London day

Grace Nichols

POEM DICTIONARY
North Circular — a busy London road

Stanley was settling in well —
he knew he'd never miss the
bustling sounds of the big city...

Grace Nichols

Once you've finished wishing you were on a Caribbean island instead of doing <u>unseen poetry</u> practice, have a go at these <u>warm-up questions</u>. When you're done, turn over the page for the <u>final poem</u> in the section.

Warm-up Questions

Q1   Briefly summarise what you think the poem is about.

Q2   Why do you think the poem starts with the one-word line "Morning"?

Q3   What is the effect of referring to the man in the poem as "island man"?

Q4   What do the lines "and island man wakes up / to the sound of blue surf / in his head" suggest about the way the man feels about his original island home?

Q5   What is the effect of repetition in the phrases "groggily groggily" and "muffling muffling"?

Q6   Describe how language relating to the sea is used to link the island and London. What effect does this have?

Q7   Identify a use of sibilance in the poem. What is its effect?

Q8   a) How does the poet use colour in the poem?

      b) How does this affect the presentation of the man's original home and London in the poem?

Q9   What is the effect of enjambment in the poem?

Q10   Why do you think the poet chose to add extra spacing before "groggily groggily" and "to surge of wheels"?

Q11   Comment on the final line of the poem, "Another London day". What effect does it have?

Section Two — Unseen Poetry Practice

Remember

Joy Harjo was born in Oklahoma in 1951. She is a poet and musician of Native American descent. A lot of her writing explores Native American culture and beliefs, as well as the effects of colonialism.

Remember

Remember the sky that you were born under,
know each of the star's stories.
Remember the moon, know who she is.
Remember the sun's birth at dawn, that is the
5   strongest point of time. Remember sundown
and the giving away to night.
Remember your birth, how your mother struggled
to give you form and breath. You are evidence of
her life, and her mother's, and hers.
10   Remember your father. He is your life, also.
Remember the earth whose skin you are:
red earth, black earth, yellow earth, white earth
brown earth, we are earth.
Remember the plants, trees, animal life who all have their
15   tribes, their families, their histories, too. Talk to them,
listen to them. They are alive poems.
Remember the wind. Remember her voice. She knows the
origin of this universe.
Remember you are all people and all people
20   are you.
Remember you are this universe and this
universe is you.
Remember all is in motion, is growing, is you.
Remember language comes from this.
25   Remember the dance language is, that life is.
Remember.

Joy Harjo

Joy Harjo

Ah, at last — you're onto the <u>final poem</u> of the section. You should know your onions when it comes to <u>analysing poetry</u> by now, but just in case you need another recap: <u>read</u>, <u>annotate</u>, <u>plan</u>, <u>answer</u>. Lovely stuff.

Warm-up Questions

Q1   Explain briefly what you think the poem is about.

Q2   What do the first two lines, "Remember the sky that you were born under, / know each of the star's stories", suggest about how a person should think about their own life?

Q3   Why do you think the poet chose to use second-person address in the poem? Explain your answer.

Q4   What is the effect of the poem being written as one continuous stanza?

Q5   Find an example of enjambment in the poem and explain its effect.

Q6   What is suggested by the sentence "You are evidence of / her life, and her mother's, and hers."?

Q7   Give an example of personification in the poem and explain why it is used by the poet.

Q8   What is the effect of the repetition of "Remember" throughout the poem?

Q9   Find an example of a metaphor in the poem. Explain what effect it creates.

Q10   How would you describe the overall mood of the poem? Explain your answer.

Exam-style Question

Compare how memory is presented in 'Island Man' and 'Remember'.
You should think about:
- the main ideas in the poems
- the form, structure and language used by the poets.

Section Three — Marking Sample Answers

Mark Scheme

I bet you've always wanted to be an examiner for the day, haven't you? Thought so. That's why I've given you a whole section where you can mark some sample exam answers. I knew you'd be pleased. But before you dive in, have a good look at these two pages...

This section lets you mark some sample answer extracts

1) Marking extracts from sample exam answers is a great way to find out exactly what you'll need to do to get the grade you want.

2) Remember, in this section you're only marking extracts, not full answers. The essays you'll write in the exam will be longer than the answer extracts on the next few pages.

3) The mark scheme on this page is similar to the one your examiner will use. The idea is for you to use it to help you mark the sample answer extracts in the rest of the section.

4) The next page has some advice about how to use the mark scheme, including some things to look out for in the sample answer extracts.

5) These extracts should give you a good idea of what the examiner will be checking for when they mark your exam answer. Don't forget, grade 9 is the top grade you can get in the exam.

6) So before you do anything else, read the mark scheme and advice, and make sure you understand them.

This is the mark scheme that you should use

Grade	Assessment Objective	What is written
8-9	AO1	• Shows an insightful and critical analysis of the poems • Critically compares a broad and varied range of similarities and/or differences between the poems • Effectively integrates a full range of precise examples to support interpretations • Convincingly explores original interpretations of ideas/themes/attitudes in the poems
	AO2	• Closely evaluates the use of language, structure and form, using technical terms effectively • Gives a detailed exploration of how the techniques used affect the reader
6-7	AO1	• Shows a carefully thought out and developed analysis of the poems • Offers a focused comparison of a wide range of similarities and/or differences between the poems • Integrates well-chosen examples to support interpretations • Carefully considers ideas/themes/attitudes in the poems, including original interpretations
	AO2	• Analyses the use of language, structure and form, using correct technical terms • Examines the way the techniques used affect the reader
4-5	AO1	• Shows an understanding of the important aspects of the poems • Makes relevant comparisons of similarities and/or differences between the poems • Provides relevant examples to support interpretations • Shows awareness of ideas/themes/attitudes in the poems, possibly offering original interpretations
	AO2	• Explains the use of language, structure and form, using some relevant terms • Comments on how some of the techniques used affect the reader

You can also be awarded grades 1-3. We haven't included any sample answer extracts at 1-3 level though — so those grades aren't in this mark scheme.

Mark Scheme

On this page are some tips on how to <u>use</u> the mark scheme on p.32, with a few things to <u>look out</u> for when you're reading the <u>sample answer extracts</u>. Take a look, then <u>flip over the page</u> to start marking...

Check that comparisons are made throughout the answer

1) When you're asked to compare poems, you need to find <u>similarities</u> and <u>differences</u> between them.

2) This means <u>both poems</u> should be discussed in <u>every paragraph</u>.

3) <u>Comparative words</u> can help to do this. They clearly show the examiner if a point being made is a <u>similarity</u> or <u>difference</u> between the two poems.

4) Here are a few <u>examples</u> of comparative words for you to look out for when <u>marking</u> the sample answer extracts:

| similarly | equally | in contrast | however | conversely |

Keep an eye out for technical terms

1) Good answers will use <u>technical terms</u> to describe the <u>techniques</u> used by the poets.

2) When you're <u>marking</u> the sample answer extracts in this section, look out for examples of <u>technical terms</u> being used.

3) The terms used must be <u>accurate</u> or they <u>won't</u> get any marks. Examiners will also be looking out for technical terms being used to help <u>support</u> and <u>explain</u> each point.

4) Here's an <u>example</u> of using technical terms correctly:

X *The poet uses words that are also sounds.*   ✓ *The poet uses <u>onomatopoeia</u>.*

Look out for quotes and examples in the answer extracts

1) When the <u>examiner</u> marks <u>your answer</u>, they will be paying close attention to whether you've used <u>quotes</u> and <u>examples</u> from the poems to <u>back up</u> your argument.

2) Think like an examiner when you're <u>marking</u> the answer extracts on the next few pages and look out for the way the extracts use <u>evidence</u> from the poems:

- The quotes and examples should have been <u>carefully</u> chosen — they must be <u>relevant</u> to the point being made.
- There's <u>no need</u> to quote <u>large chunks</u> of text.
- <u>Exact</u> quotes should be inside <u>quotation marks</u> (" ") like this: "The wind howled down the valley."
- If the text has been <u>rephrased</u>, you don't need quotation marks.

  E.g.   The wind is very loud in the valley.

- Wherever possible, quotes should be integrated into the sentences so that the <u>writing flows</u> nicely.

  E.g.   The personification in "The wind howled down the valley" emphasises how loud the wind is.

Listen Mr Oxford Don — John Agard

John Agard was born in <u>Guyana, South America</u>. He then moved to <u>Britain</u> in 1977. The <u>sample answer</u> <u>extracts</u> for this question for you to mark are on <u>p.36-37</u>, so head over there once you've read these poems.

Q1   Compare how the writers of 'Listen Mr Oxford Don' and 'Neighbours' present ideas about prejudice.

You should write about:
- the main ideas in the poems
- the language used by the poets
- the form and structure used by the poets.

Support your comparisons by using evidence from the poems.

(20 marks)

Listen Mr Oxford Don

Me not no Oxford don
me a simple immigrant
from Clapham Common
I didn't graduate
5 I immigrate

But listen Mr Oxford don
I'm a man on de run
and a man on de run
is a dangerous one

10 I ent have no gun
I ent have no knife
but mugging de Queen's English
is the story of my life

I don't need no axe
15 to split/ up yu syntax
I don't need no hammer
to mash/ up yu grammar

I warning you Mr Oxford don
I'm a wanted man
20 and a wanted man
is a dangerous one

Dem accuse me of assault
on de Oxford dictionary/
imagine a concise peaceful man like me/
25 dem want me serve time
for inciting rhyme to riot
but I tekking it quiet
down here in Clapham Common

I'm not a violent man Mr Oxford don
30 I only armed wit mih human breath
but human breath
is a dangerous weapon

So mek dem send one big word after me
I ent serving no jail sentence
35 I slashing suffix in self-defence
I bashing future wit present tense
and if necessary

I making de Queen's English accessory/ to my offence

John Agard

Here's a man who *does* need an axe.

Section Three — Marking Sample Answers

Neighbours — Benjamin Zephaniah

Benjamin Zephaniah was born in Birmingham in 1958. His parents are from the Caribbean and his poetry is influenced by his Jamaican heritage. His poems often use humour to address serious issues such as racism.

Neighbours

I am the type you are supposed
to fear
Black and foreign
Big and dreadlocks
5   An uneducated grass eater.

I talk in tongues
I chant at night
I appear anywhere,
I sleep with lions
10   And when the moon gets me
I am a Wailer.

I am moving in
Next door to you
So you can get to know me,
15   You will see my shadow
In the bathroom window,
My aromas will occupy
Your space,
Our ball will be in your court.
20   How will you feel?

You should feel good
You have been chosen.

I am the type you are supposed
to love
25   Dark and mysterious
Tall and natural
Thinking, tea total.
I talk in schools
I sing on TV
30   I am in the papers,
I keep cool cats

And when the sun is shining
I go Carnival.

They do look quite cuddly,
but I wouldn't advise
having a snuggle.

Benjamin Zephaniah

Section Three — Marking Sample Answers

2

Sample Answers

Here are the sample answer extracts for the question on p.34. For each one, think about where it fits in the mark scheme on p.32. Most answers won't fit perfectly into one band, so concentrate on finding the best fit.

Sample Answer Extract 1

Both poets use the structure of their poems to challenge prejudice. For example, the first stanza of 'Listen Mr Oxford Don' has a calm tone, created by the way the narrator casts himself as a "simple immigrant" compared to the Oxford don, and how he seems to accept this. However, the tone becomes more forceful in the second stanza when the narrator firmly tells the Oxford don to "listen". This shift in tone is emphasised through the repetition of "a man on de run" and the heavy alliterative 'd' sounds, which show how the narrator changes and challenges the idea of the "simple immigrant". 'Neighbours' is structured differently in that the first two stanzas address the negative opinions that people might have of the narrator. These are then directly reversed in the last two stanzas. For example, "I talk in tongues" becomes "I talk in schools". Speaking in "tongues" suggests the narrator is mysterious and not easily understood, whereas by describing how they "talk in schools", they are presented as familiar and easily understood, even by children. The use of anaphora draws attention to this contrast and emphasises how people's assumptions can be wrong. Structuring the poem in this way allows the poet to counter people's prejudices and makes the reader challenge their own prejudices.

a) Write down the grade band (4-5, 6-7 or 8-9) that you think this answer falls into.
b) Give at least two reasons why you chose that grade.

Sample Answer Extract 2

Both poems show how people often have incorrect opinions about people from different backgrounds and cultures. 'Listen Mr Oxford Don' uses language of crime and violence to show how people think immigrants are aggressive. However, the narrator shows that this is not true when he says he doesn't have a gun or a knife, which proves that he is not violent. This shows that people's opinions can often be wrong.

Similarly, 'Neighbours' uses phrases that greatly contrast in how they portray people from different backgrounds and cultures. In the second stanza, the narrator says that they have slept with lions. This is a dangerous activity and makes the narrator seem different when compared to most people. However, when the narrator later says "I keep cool cats", it makes them seem much friendlier. This shows that people shouldn't be afraid of the narrator.

a) Write down the grade band (4-5, 6-7 or 8-9) that you think this answer falls into.
b) Give at least two reasons why you chose that grade.

Section Three — Marking Sample Answers

Sample Answers

Sample Answer Extract 3

In the poems, both narrators address someone directly to get across their argument. Agard's narrator talks to a "Mr Oxford don", who stands for British culture and the people who may be prejudiced against the narrator. The narrator is bold when he tells the Oxford don to "listen" to him. The title also makes it clear the narrator is talking to the Oxford don. This direct address demonstrates that he is standing up to people who are prejudiced. 'Neighbours' is slightly different in that the narrator talks to the reader instead. They ask "How will you feel?" when they move in next door, which makes the reader think more about their own prejudices. The narrator also says that "you can get to know me", which shows that they are trying to tackle prejudice by bringing people together and encouraging them to get to know each other. When they say "You should feel good / You have been chosen", they seem to be saying to the reader that they have won something. This suggests that the narrator feels that living alongside people from different backgrounds and cultures is positive rather than negative.

a) Write down the grade band (4-5, 6-7 or 8-9) that you think this answer falls into.

b) Give at least two reasons why you chose that grade.

Sample Answer Extract 4

Both poets use contrasting imagery to challenge views that people might have of immigrants. In 'Listen Mr Oxford Don', violent images of a "gun" and a "knife" contrast with more peaceful imagery, such as the narrator being "only armed wit mih human breath". Compared to these weapons, which are hard, solid and cold, the image of "breath" is light, airy and harmless. This makes the narrator seem gentle and reflects the poem's overall message that he isn't harming the English language as some people might believe, but that his way of speaking is just as valid as "de Queen's English".

'Neighbours' also features contrasting imagery to show that people's perceptions of immigrants are often incorrect and based on assumptions. The poet directly contrasts the threatening image created in the reader's mind by "Black and foreign / Big and dreadlocks" with "Dark and mysterious / Tall and natural". Similarly, the poet contrasts the image of the narrator as a "Wailer", where they are affected by the moon, with the image of how they "go Carnival" when "the sun is shining". The poet uses this second image and the positive connotations of the sun, like brightness and light, to show the narrator as a positive figure. These contrasts emphasise the poet's message that the narrator isn't dangerous or threatening as some people may believe.

a) Write down the grade band (4-5, 6-7 or 8-9) that you think this answer falls into.

b) Give at least two reasons why you chose that grade.

Introduction to Poetry — Billy Collins

Billy Collins was born in 1941 in New York City. He has served as both the US Poet Laureate and New York State Poet Laureate, as well as being a university professor. That's an impressive C.V. right there.

Q2 Compare how the writers of 'Introduction to Poetry' and 'Volumes' present feelings about reading.

You should write about:
- the main ideas in the poems
- the language used by the poets
- the form and structure used by the poets.

Support your comparisons by using evidence from the poems.

(20 marks)

The sample answers for this question are on p.40-41.

Introduction to Poetry

I ask them to take a poem
and hold it up to the light
like a color slide

or press an ear against its hive.

5   I say drop a mouse into a poem
and watch him probe his way out,

or walk inside the poem's room
and feel the walls for a light switch.

I want them to waterski
10   across the surface of a poem
waving at the author's name on the shore.

But all they want to do
is tie the poem to a chair with rope
and torture a confession out of it.

15   They begin beating it with a hose
to find out what it really means.

Billy Collins

POEM DICTIONARY
slide — a piece of photograph film that
   can be projected onto a screen.

Mandy wasn't sure trying to
wave towards the shore was
such a good idea.

Section Three — Marking Sample Answers

Volumes — Jo Shapcott

Jo Shapcott was born in 1953 in London and grew up in Hemel Hempstead. She has taught at several UK universities and has won many awards for her work, including the Queen's Gold Medal for Poetry.

Volumes

They put me in a fever. It's not enough
to look. I want to hold them all
and stuff them in the gaps in my head.
I gallop past Health towards Travel
5   where I break into a muck sweat
as I lift and sniff a book about Verona.
The odour makes me stagger and long
to be a book mite, to live right inside
and gulp holes through the picture maps.
10   I don't trust myself in Fiction. The thought
of those thousands and thousands of stories —
the crush and babble of other minds —
makes the whites of my eyes show and roll.
Last time I sauntered by those shelves
15   I slammed into the New Titles display
and crashed right through a pyramid of books
on to my back among the toppled photos
of authors winking at the carry on.
I got a cuppa and a pat on the rump
20   from the kind saleslady who has the bubble
of book hysteria herself, I'd guess.
If she could, she'd wear print on her skin.
There are words written for everything,
I think, and it's only a matter of time
25   before I find a new 'How To' book:
how to stand upright, how not to fall
and how not to cry out when you do.

Jo Shapcott

Sample Answers

These are the sample answer extracts for the question on p.38. Have a try at giving them a grade by using the mark scheme on p.32. Remember to explain what's wrong with the answer as well as what's right.

Sample Answer Extract 1

Both narrators want to explore books or poems deeply. The narrator of 'Introduction to Poetry' describes a poem as a room that students should walk inside and explore, suggesting that the best way to understand a poem is to see it from the inside. They also say that the reader should try to turn on a "light switch" inside the poem to make its meaning clear.

Similarly, the narrator of 'Volumes' says that they want to be a "mite" and "live right inside" books. This shows how strong the narrator's love for reading is. The narrator of 'Volumes' also describes their love of reading using the language of illness — they say that books give them a "fever" and talk about "book hysteria". This shows that the narrator loves reading so much that it has made them ill and unable to think clearly. This may have the effect of making the reader think that a love of reading is a sort of sickness or even madness.

    a)   Write down the grade band (4-5, 6-7 or 8-9) that you think this answer falls into.

    b)   Give at least two reasons why you chose that grade.

Sample Answer Extract 2

Both poems use form and structure to present the narrators' feelings about reading. Collins' poem is written in free verse with seven short stanzas. The lack of a regular rhyme scheme and metre makes it sound natural, encouraging the reader to relate to the narrator's message by presenting it as personal. However, iambic tetrameter is sometimes used, such as in "or press an ear against its hive". Here the reader can hear the change in metre and so is made actively aware of the poet's message in these words about the importance of listening to the sound of a poem. 'Volumes' also has no regular rhyme scheme or metre, but whereas Collins uses free verse to make his poem sound natural, Shapcott combines it with a lack of stanza breaks to make her poem seem chaotic. This has the effect of causing the reader to read quickly without pausing, mirroring the crazed "fever" the narrator experiences when surrounded by books. This effect is increased by the frequent use of enjambment, such as "It's not enough / to look", which emphasises the words "not enough" to the reader. Enjambment has a similar effect in the phrase "The thought / of those thousands and thousands of stories", where the phrase "The thought" is emphasised, suggesting that just the idea of how many books there are is overwhelming. Both these examples suggest that the narrator is affected deeply by the sheer number of books and how much they want to read them.

    a)   Write down the grade band (4-5, 6-7 or 8-9) that you think this answer falls into.

    b)   Give at least two reasons why you chose that grade.

Sample Answers

Sample Answer Extract 3

Whereas 'Introduction to Poetry' is concerned with how a poem should be read, 'Volumes' is about its narrator's extreme love of reading. The different use of language in the poems reflects their different focuses. 'Introduction to Poetry' uses several vivid images to suggest to the reader that poems should be approached in multiple ways in order to understand them fully. For example, the narrator describes looking at a poem "like a color slide", and using touch to "feel the walls". These metaphorical, sensory descriptions portray poetry as varied and complex, which emphasises to the reader the narrator's message that poems must be explored from a variety of angles in order to be understood. The poet then goes on to describe waterskiing "across the surface of a poem". Here, "surface" has a double meaning: it refers to both the surface of the water and the 'surface' meaning of a poem. This wordplay therefore also conveys the value of a superficial response to a poem. The use of language in 'Volumes' is somewhat different, as the poet uses a series of strong verbs to convey the narrator's powerful reaction to books. Words like "gallop", "stagger", "gulp", "slammed" and "crashed" communicate the strength of the narrator's reaction. The physical nature of these verbs, reinforced by their heavy consonant sounds, like 'st' and 'cr', expresses how, for the narrator, their love for books is felt on a deep physical level. This presents an image of an uncontrolled, overwhelming devotion to reading.

a)   Write down the grade band (4-5, 6-7 or 8-9) that you think this answer falls into.

b)   Give at least two reasons why you chose that grade.

Sample Answer Extract 4

'Introduction to Poetry' uses personification to portray a poem as a person experiencing torture. The poet uses the image of a poem being tied "to a chair with rope" as well as words like "beating" — both this image and these words are violent. This use of personification forces the reader to respond negatively to the manner of reading a poem described in these stanzas, partly because of the violence and partly because they are more likely to feel sympathy for a human.

'Volumes', on the other hand, uses animal imagery to express the narrator's love of books. For example, the narrator "gallop[s]" and "break[s] into a muck sweat", which makes them sound like a horse. This animal imagery conveys to the reader the narrator's uncontrollable excitement about books and reading. The narrator also describes how they want to "sniff" a book about Verona. This makes them seem like a dog and represents how they want to absorb the book in every way possible. This emphasises how important books are to the narrator.

a)   Write down the grade band (4-5, 6-7 or 8-9) that you think this answer falls into.

b)   Give at least two reasons why you chose that grade.

Below the Green Corrie — Norman MacCaig

Norman MacCaig (1910-1996) was a Scottish poet born in Edinburgh. He taught at the University of Stirling and published many collections of poetry during his lifetime. In 1979 he was awarded an OBE.

Q3   Compare how the writers of 'Below the Green Corrie'
and 'The Moment' present nature.

You should write about:
- the main ideas in the poems
- the language used by the poets
- the form and structure used by the poets.

Support your comparisons by using evidence from the poems.

(20 marks)

The sample answers for this question are on p.44-45.

Below the Green Corrie

The mountains gathered round me
like bandits. Their leader
swaggered up close in the dark light,
full of threats, full of thunders.

5   But it was they who stood and delivered.
They gave me their money and their lives.
They filled me with mountains and thunders.
My life was enriched
with an infusion of theirs.

10   I clambered downhill through the ugly weather.
And when I turned to look goodbye
to those marvellous prowlers
a sunshaft had pierced the clouds
and their leader,
15   that swashbuckling mountain,
was wearing
a bandolier of light.

Norman MacCaig

POEM DICTIONARY
corrie — a hollow on a mountainside
stood and delivered — referring to a command used by highwaymen (robbers who
                 targeted travellers) to get victims to hand over valuables.
infusion — a mix or blend
prowler — something which prowls, i.e. moves stealthily
sunshaft — a ray of sunlight
swashbuckling — wild, adventurous
bandolier — an over-the-shoulder belt used to hold gun cartridges

'Oi, pal — what you lookin' at?!'

Section Three — Marking Sample Answers

The Moment — Margaret Atwood

Margaret Atwood was born in 1939 in Canada and began writing plays and poems at six years old. Her published work includes poems, novels and essays, and she has won many awards for her writing.

The Moment

The moment when, after many years
of hard work and a long voyage
you stand in the centre of your room,
house, half-acre, square mile, island, country,
5   knowing at last how you got there,
and say, *I own this*,

is the same moment when the trees unloose
their soft arms from around you,
the birds take back their language,
10   the cliffs fissure and collapse,
the air moves back from you like a wave
and you can't breathe.

No, they whisper. *You own nothing.*
You were a visitor, time after time
15   *climbing the hill, planting the flag, proclaiming.*
We never belonged to you.
You never found us.
It was always the other way round.

Margaret Atwood

POEM DICTIONARY
half-acre — a measure of land size
square mile — a measure of land size equal to 640 acres
fissure — split
planting the flag — placing a flag on an area of land to claim
            ownership of it or show it has been conquered.

Sample Answers

This is the <u>last</u> set of <u>sample answer extracts</u> to mark, to go with the question on <u>p.42</u>. Take a look, then give them a grade using the mark scheme on <u>p.32</u> for guidance. Then you can take your examiner's hat off.

Sample Answer Extract 1

> Both poems use language to show that nature can be both violent and also beautiful or gentle. MacCaig uses the language of stories about highwaymen, like "swashbuckling", "bandolier" and "stood and delivered", to present the mountains as exciting but also powerful and potentially dangerous. However, he also describes them positively by saying that the narrator was "enriched" by them, and by describing them as lit up by the sun. This use of a beautiful image shows the reader the narrator's admiration for the mountains and for nature. Similarly, in 'The Moment', nature is presented in a way that conveys to the reader that it can be a threatening force. For example, the line "the cliffs fissure and collapse" uses strong, forceful verbs to portray the violence of nature. This contrasts with the quiet of the third stanza, where nature doesn't shout, but whispers. Both poems therefore suggest that nature can behave in different ways — in Atwood's poem, it is implied that nature is only violent to those who try to control it.

a)   Write down the grade band (4-5, 6-7 or 8-9) that you think this answer falls into.

b)   Give at least two reasons why you chose that grade.

Sample Answer Extract 2

> Both poems use personification to convey their narrator's feelings about nature to the reader. In 'Below the Green Corrie', the mountains are personified as bandits through phrases like "gathered round me / like bandits" and "wearing / a bandolier of light". The personification used by MacCaig here shows that the narrator is both fearful and in awe of the mountains. This technique therefore helps to communicate to the reader the narrator's emotions about nature.
>
> 'The Moment' also uses personification, but does so to explore the connection between people and nature. For example, the trees are described as removing their "soft arms" from around the reader, which suggests that they are taking away their love and protection. This is described as taking place when ownership is declared over nature, as in the phrase "*I own this*". This suggests that personification is being used in the poem to represent the way people lose a positive, loving connection with nature when they try to own it — the technique gives the reader a vivid sense of the negative consequences of taking a possessive, inconsiderate approach to nature.

a)   Write down the grade band (4-5, 6-7 or 8-9) that you think this answer falls into.

b)   Give at least two reasons why you chose that grade.

Sample Answers

Sample Answer Extract 3

Form and structure are used in both poems to present nature's relationship with humans. 'Below the Green Corrie' uses end-stopping to convey a change in the relationship between the narrator and the mountains. Unlike the more enjambed first stanza, the second stanza includes three short, end-stopped lines, for example "But it was they who stood and delivered." and "They filled me with mountains and thunders." The poet emphasises this change of direction from the first stanza to the second by using the conjunction "But" at the beginning of the second stanza. The sense of completeness created by this end-stopping emphasises the surprising contrast between nature's behaviour in the two stanzas and shows how the human now holds a position of control in the relationship. 'The Moment' uses similar aspects of form and structure, with the first two stanzas written as one long, enjambed sentence, suggesting the inevitability of nature's reaction to the human claim of ownership. This sense of inevitability is reinforced by the way the first stanza ends with the phrase "*I own this*" and the second with "and you can't breathe", as this suggests that it is the human claim of ownership over nature which causes nature's violent reaction. These stanzas contrast with the third stanza, which is heavily end-stopped and uses short sentences. These techniques lend nature's statements a powerful sense of finality, such as with "We never belonged to you." This emphasises to the reader that it is nature that is in control of humans, and not the other way around.

a) Write down the grade band (4-5, 6-7 or 8-9) that you think this answer falls into.

b) Give at least two reasons why you chose that grade.

Sample Answer Extract 4

Both poets present nature as a very powerful force. In 'Below the Green Corrie', nature is shown to be a threatening force when the mountains are presented using the simile "like bandits". The poet also describes them as being "full of threats". The language the poet uses here is related to criminals and lawlessness. This might make the reader feel frightened of or intimidated by the mountains, as it suggests that they are somehow dangerous.

This is similar to the way that Atwood presents nature in 'The Moment'. In this poem, the narrator says that the reader might say "*I own this*". Later on in the poem, however, nature speaks back and says "*You own nothing*" and "*We never belonged to you*". This shows that nature is the one that is really in control and that humans are less powerful than nature. This reminds the reader of the poet's message that people shouldn't try to control nature.

a) Write down the grade band (4-5, 6-7 or 8-9) that you think this answer falls into.

b) Give at least two reasons why you chose that grade.

Those Winter Sundays — Robert Hayden

Here's your first <u>sample exam</u> — hooray. You'll have <u>45 minutes</u> to answer the <u>question</u> in the exam. This includes reading and annotating the poems and planning your answer, so you'll need to <u>use your time</u> wisely.

> **Q1**   Compare how the writers of 'Those Winter Sundays' and 'My Father on His Shield' present the relationship between a father and his child.
>
> You should write about:
> - the main ideas in the poems
> - the language used by the poets
> - the form and structure used by the poets.
>
> Support your comparisons by using evidence from the poems.
>
>   **(20 marks)**

Those Winter Sundays

Sundays too my father got up early
and put his clothes on in the blueblack cold,
then with cracked hands that ached
from labor in the weekday weather made
5   banked fires blaze. No one ever thanked him.

I'd wake and hear the cold splintering, breaking.
When the rooms were warm, he'd call,
and slowly I would rise and dress,
fearing the chronic angers of that house,

10   Speaking indifferently to him,
who had driven out the cold
and polished my good shoes as well.
What did I know, what did I know
of love's austere and lonely offices?

Robert Hayden

<u>POEM DICTIONARY</u>
offices — can mean duties or obligations as well as places of work

My Father on His Shield — Walt McDonald

My Father on His Shield

Shiny as wax, the cracked veneer Scotch-taped
and brittle. I can't bring my father back.
Legs crossed, he sits there brash

5   with a private's stripe, a world away
from the war they would ship him to
within days. Cannons flank his face

and banners above him like the flag
my mother kept on the mantel, folded tight,
white stars sharp-pointed on a field of blue.

10   I remember his fists, the iron he pounded,
five-pound hammer ringing steel,
the frame he made for a sled that winter

before the war. I remember the rope in his fist
around my chest, his other fist
15   shoving the snow, and downhill we dived,

his boots by my boots on the tongue,
pines whishing by, ice in my eyes, blinking
and squealing. I remember the troop train,

steam billowing like a smoke screen.
20   I remember wrecking the sled weeks later
and pounding to beat the iron flat,

but it stayed there bent
and stacked in the barn by the anvil,
and I can't bring him back.

Walt McDonald

Flowers — Wendy Cope

Just what you've always wanted — another sample exam. I know you can't wait to get started, but make sure you analyse both poems and jot down a quick essay plan before you get stuck into your answer.

Q2   Compare how the writers of 'Flowers' and 'Don't Say I Said' present the end of a relationship.

You should write about:
- the main ideas in the poems
- the language used by the poets
- the form and structure used by the poets.

Support your comparisons by using evidence from the poems.

(20 marks)

Flowers

Some men never think of it.
You did. You'd come along
And say you'd nearly brought me flowers
But something had gone wrong.

5   The shop was closed. Or you had doubts —
The sort that minds like ours
Dream up incessantly. You thought
I might not want your flowers.

It made me smile and hug you then.
10   Now I can only smile.
But, look, the flowers you nearly brought
Have lasted all this while.

Wendy Cope

Don't Say I Said — Sophie Hannah

Don't Say I Said

Next time you speak to you-know-who
I've got a message for him.
Tell him that I have lost a stone
Since the last time I saw him.
5   Tell him that I've got three new books
Coming out soon, but play it
Cool, make it sound spontaneous.
Don't say I said to say it.

He might ask if I've mentioned him.
10   Say I have once, in passing.
Memorize everything he says
And, no, it won't be grassing
When you repeat his words to me –
It's the only way to play it.
15   Tell him I'm toned and tanned and fine.
Don't say I said to say it.

Say that serenity and grace
Have taken root inside me.
My top-note is frivolity
20   But beneath, dark passions guide me.
Tell him I'm radiant and replete
And add that every day it
Seems I am harder to resist.
Don't say I said to say it.

25   Tell him that all my ancient faults
Have been eradicated.
I do not carp or analyse
As I might have when we dated.
Say I'm not bossy any more
30   Or, better still, convey it
Subtly, but get the point across.
Don't say I said to say it.

Sophie Hannah

Answers

Section Two — Unseen Poetry Practice

Page 9 — Handbag

Q1   The narrator is describing their mother's old handbag and the things she used to carry in it, including letters from the narrator's father, mints, lipstick and Coty powder.

Q2   The narrator may be looking through their mother's handbag because their mother has recently died. The smells of the handbag are still strong, suggesting that it was used fairly recently, but the fact that the narrator is looking through it, and the vivid memories evoked by doing so, suggest that their mother is no longer alive.

Q3   The poem shows the mother's love for her husband by emphasising the importance of his letters to her. It also describes the mother's "anguish", which is linked to her husband's absence — possibly his death — during the war. The slow rhythm of the poem and the strong memories it describes suggest that the narrator feels sad and wistful as they think about their mother.

Q4   This phrase suggests that the letters were so important to the mother that she filled her handbag with them. It may also hint at the mother's loneliness, suggesting that her life was "crowded" with letters and the memories they contained, rather than being filled with relationships with the people around her.

Q5   The use of enjambment here emphasises the phrase "all through the war". This suggests the impact of the war on the narrator's mother, and also indicates the importance of these letters to her during the war — perhaps the mother saw them as a sort of charm to ensure her husband would come home.

Q6   The poet mentions several very distinctive smells, such as "mints", "Coty powder" and "leather", to create a sense of how the handbag smells. The use of enjambment emphasises the words "smell" and "Odour", showing how powerful the narrator finds these smells. They are important to the narrator because they are strongly associated with the way they remember their mother — her "womanliness" — and because they bring back vivid memories.

Q7   Specifying the brand of face powder emphasises that this is a memory of a specific person and time period. It helps the reader appreciate the sense

of nostalgia the handbag brings for the narrator, because the narrator can remember such small details so closely.

Q8   The poet uses touch to describe the way the narrator's mother treated her husband's letters, and to show how valuable they were to her. The word "softened" shows how often she looked at them, while the verbs "opened" and "refolded" emphasise how carefully she handled them.

Q9   This makes the sentence stand out, so that it catches the eye, even when you just glance at the poem. This technique emphasises the importance of the letters. It suggests that the letters may have dominated the mother's life, making them stand out in the narrator's memories of her, in the same way that this sentence stands out on the page.

Q10 This use of repetition slows the pace of the poem, and emphasises the words "womanliness", "love", "anguish" and "war". This shows how important these concepts are in the narrator's memories of their mother, and creates a contrast between the two positive words and the two negative ones.

Q11 The poem's lack of a rhyme scheme makes it seem wistful and melancholy. It creates the impression that the poem records the narrator's train of thought, which makes it seem very personal.

Page 11 — Jumper

Q1   The narrator remembers how their mother used to knit in their bomb shelter during the war, and how she used knitting to give her family courage.

Q2   The narrator says that bombs fell "round our home", so they must have been quite close. The bombs sent "shivers through the walls", reinforcing the image in "walls shake" — the walls physically shook with the impact of the explosions.

Q3   The narrator's mother made her "scared child" hold the wool as a way of distracting them from the bombs. The child could concentrate on holding the wool instead of thinking about the bombs. It also gave the child a strong link with their mother, which would have reassured them.

Q4   The first emotion in the poem is fear, when the narrator talks about being a "scared child" in the bomb shelter. The second main emotion is the admiration the narrator now feels for their mother's "composure" when she was faced with death. The poet shows these emotions by highlighting the mother's bravery and its effect on the narrator in both the past and the present.

Q5   The poet says the people in the shelter "shivered" and that the bombs made the walls "shiver". The comparison

personifies the walls, making it seem like they're also afraid of the bombs.

Q6   a)   The first twelve lines describe the narrator's memories of their mother when they were a child. The last four lines move to the present day.

     b)   The narrator uses the memory of their mother from childhood to highlight her courage in later years, when she was approaching death.

Q7   The poet describes the sound ("click of needles") and feel of the shelter ("cold" with shaking walls) to create a vivid image that helps transport the reader into the scene. The use of the senses makes the scene seem more real to the reader.

Q8   The bombs are described as "whistling". This helps the reader imagine the sound of them falling, and the narrator's fear.

Q9   The rhythm of the poem is quite regular, which brings to mind the rhythmic sound of the narrator's mother knitting.

Q10 The jumper is "shop-bought" because the mother realised that she was too frail to knit one herself. It is "black", which is the colour of mourning — this implies she knew she would die soon when she bought it. Separating the last line emphasises the contrast with the mother's knitting and recreates the shock of opening the present.

Exam-style Question

You'll need to spend about 45 minutes on this, and your answer will probably bring in some of the things you thought about when you answered the other questions on the two poems. These are some points you could mention:

• Both poets use an object to give the reader a clear sense of each narrator's memories of and feelings about their mother. In Fainlight's poem, the contents of the handbag represent the narrator's memories of their mother, especially their mother's love for her husband. The jumper in Harrison's poem represents the narrator's mother's courage during the war, as well as her role as a source of comfort and practicality in times of crisis.

• The mothers in each poem are portrayed quite differently. In Harrison's poem, the narrator's mother seems strong and courageous. The "steady" clicking of her knitting needles shows how she was undisturbed by the sound of bombs outside and symbolises the steadying influence she had on the narrator. This contrasts with the "anguish" associated with the mother in 'Handbag'. This anguish is mentioned in the summary of the bag's "Odour", which implies that it is part of the narrator's lasting impression of their mother. It suggests to the reader that the torment caused by the loss of the

Answers

narrator's father was a large aspect of the mother's life.

- Both poems use the senses to convey the narrators' vivid memories about items associated with their mothers. In 'Handbag', the poet describes the very specific smell of the handbag — of "mints / and lipstick and Coty powder". This emphasises how familiar the narrator is with the handbag, because they can recall exactly how it smells. In 'Jumper', the poet uses the onomatopoeia of the word "click" to clearly convey the sound of the mother's knitting needles. This helps the reader to imagine what the narrator could hear and understand the calming effect that it had on them.

- The poems both use repetition. In 'Handbag', repetition of the word "letters" emphasises to the reader how important the "Letters from my father" were to the narrator's mother, and how they dominate the narrator's memories of her. Similarly, in 'Jumper', the word "bombs" is repeated at random points, echoing the random explosions of bombs during the war. This helps the reader to understand the danger the family faced and the mother's courage in facing it so "calmly".

- The two poems use rhyme and rhythm in different ways. The use of enjambment in 'Handbag' gives the poem a slow rhythm, which seems wistful and melancholy, while the lack of rhyme makes the poem seem natural and personal. This reflects the narrator's own sadness when they look back on their mother's life and her suffering during the war. In contrast, in 'Jumper', the regular rhyme scheme creates an even rhythm, which mirrors the sound of the mother's knitting needles. This emphasises the narrator's admiration for the calm way their mother carried on knitting as "German bombs fell".

- The tone in 'Handbag' remains wistful and nostalgic throughout — the narrator describes the "smell" of their mother's handbag at the beginning of the poem and also at the end, when they refer to "Odour / of leather and powder". This shows the reader how the narrator is continuing to reflect upon their memories of their mother. In contrast, the separation of the final line in 'Jumper' signals a change in tone as well as a jump in time from past memories to the present. This abrupt end to the poem causes the reader to feel shocked and mirrors the narrator's shock when they opened the present.

Page 13 — At Sea

Q1 The poem is about a woman who is left behind in her home, waiting for someone she lives with to return.

Q2 The main feeling of the first stanza is boredom. The poet portrays this by describing how the woman has "nothing to do" and so she just "dusts the house" and "sweeps the bleached verandah". The woman's cleaning also shows she feels anxious — she cannot sit still and tries to keep busy. But the cleaning is futile; the broom "leaves a trail of grit". This could show that she can't cleanse her mind of her fear and anxiety.

Q3 The first stanza contains lots of 's' sounds — "dusts", "sweeps", "sand", "step", "sprinkling" and "hangs". This makes the stanza feel longer, reflecting the woman's feelings about how time slows down whilst she's alone. The sibilance also sounds like the sea, so it's a constant reminder of the woman's enemy.

Q4 The coat that the woman uses for a pillow could be the man's coat. Sleeping with the coat could help the woman to feel closer to him, and help her to feel reassured that he will return to her. She may also be waiting up for the man, so might be reluctant to go to bed properly.

Q5 The word "loathed" expresses the woman's fear and hatred of the sea — in her nightmare, she dreams that it is invading her house like a dangerous enemy. The ocean is the reason she is separated from the man, and it presents a danger to him, so she may loathe the ocean because it is the cause of her misery.

Q6 In the second stanza, the ocean is personified as entering the woman's home by "climbing the cliffs, / creeping in through the door". This makes the sea seem hostile, as if it is creeping up on her to steal away the man she is waiting for. The personification suggests that the woman feels threatened by the ocean, and reflects how powerless the sea makes her feel.

Q7 In the final stanza, the onomatopoeic sound of the "screaming" gulls creates a vivid image in the mind of the reader and gives a nightmarish quality to the poem. It's also a stark contrast to the silence of the rest of the poem, where the only sounds are the sweeping of the broom and the sibilance of the sea creeping closer. The screaming gulls might also be reminiscent of the screams of drowning sailors, highlighting the woman's fear that the man she is waiting for will die at sea.

Q8 By the end of the poem, the woman's feelings of unease have intensified. In the last two lines, the woman feels the "high tide's breakers' / chill in her arms". This cold, wet image creates a negative mood that reflects the woman's fear and unhappiness, and suggests the "loathed ocean"

has taken over her home as she feared it would. The "chill" of the waves also seems like a forewarning of death. It's as if she's holding the man's cold, drowned body in her arms, which emphasises the sense of unease in this part of the poem.

Q9 The rhythm throughout the poem is erratic, with no rhyme scheme, reflecting the woman's anxious state of mind and her urge to keep doing things to keep busy. The final stanza is heavily enjambed, which creates a feeling of time moving faster and of disorder and confusion, emphasising the woman's deteriorating state of mind as a feeling of dread sweeps over her.

Q10 The structure of the poem mimics the structure of the woman's life whilst the man is away — it's divided into day, night, day, across the three stanzas. This allows the reader to follow her experience over this time period and understand more deeply her feelings of monotony and fear.

Q11 The title 'At Sea' suggests that the absent man in the poem may be out at sea in a boat, and emphasises how much the woman is thinking about him. It may also refer to how the woman feels 'at sea' (lost and alone) without him, emphasising her strong sense of his absence.

Page 15 — The Sea

Q1 The poem is about the sea and its behaviour at different times of the day and the year, including when it is rough and when it is calm.

Q2 a) The metaphor likens the power and energy of the sea to the hunger and enthusiasm of a dog, by describing how the 'dog' "gnaws" on stones and "bounds to his feet". It also shows how the sea can sometimes be calm and quiet, like a sleeping dog.

b) The metaphor is effective because it shows the changeable nature of the sea through a dog's personality and behaviour at different times.

Q3 The 'dog' gnawing at the "rumbling, tumbling stones" represents the sea moving the stones on the beach as it moves in and out. The 'dog's' gnawing helps the reader imagine the sound of the stones as they rub and grind against each other. It may also suggest the gradual erosion of the stones into sand due to the effect of the sea.

Q4 The repetition of the word "bones" imitates the repetitive, moaning sound of the sea, making it easier for the reader to imagine its movement and the sound it makes. It also suggests that the 'dog' is desperate for food, which emphasises its hunger and hints at the dangerous nature of the sea.

Answers

Q5 The alliteration in the second stanza, for example the repetition of 'h' and 'l' in "howls and hollos long and loud", mimics the repetitive, relentless sounds being made by the 'dog'. This gives the reader a clear sense of what the sea sounded like during the stormy night.

Q6 In the first stanza, the mood is uneasy and disturbed due to the description of the way the 'dog' "moans" and "gnaws" — these painful-sounding verbs give the stanza a negative tone. In the second stanza, the mood becomes more intense as the weather gets stormier ("the night wind roars") and the sea becomes more dangerous — the 'dog' shakes water all over the cliffs, representing the spray from a rough sea. The third stanza, set in the warmer months, is much calmer, and the 'dog's' "quiet" sleepiness makes the mood softer and more relaxed.

Q7 Sibilance is used in the poem to mimic the sounds of the sea and create mood. For example, in the final stanza, the sibilance of "sandy shores", "so", and "scarcely snores" has a calming effect. It sounds soothing, helping to express the calmness of the summer scene. It also mimics the sound of a snoring dog, helping the reader imagine the soft sound of the sea.

Q8 The lines in the poem often rhyme, such as lines 2 and 3, which end with "grey" and "day", but the poem doesn't follow a consistent rhyme scheme. This reflects how the movement of the sea is generally repetitive, but unpredictable when the weather is bad. In the third stanza, the rhyme scheme is more regular, as the stanza is split into two rhyming triplets. This emphasises the calmer tone of the stanza and the more predictable movement of the gentler sea.

Q9 The poet appears to be trying to portray the sea's good and bad qualities and emphasise how varied it can be. In the first two stanzas it is wild and dangerous, but in the last stanza it is much softer, with the image of barely moving "grasses on the dune" creating a pleasant beach image. The fact that a dog — often a beloved family pet — is used as the metaphor for the sea suggests that the poet views the sea in a positive light overall, seeing its changeability as part of its nature rather than something negative.

Exam-style Question

You'll need to spend about 45 minutes on this, and your answer will probably bring in some of the things you thought about when you answered the other questions on the two poems. These are some points you could mention:

- 'At Sea' is about one woman's personal relationship with the sea as she waits at home for the man she lives with to return, including her fear of its power and potential danger. 'The Sea', in contrast, is about the ocean in a more general sense, including its behaviour at different times of the year — for example its unpredictable nature in stormy weather — and how it looks and sounds. These different focuses are conveyed by the poets' use of language, form and structure in their poems.

- The narrators of both poems present the sea as potentially dangerous. The woman in Copley's poem has a nightmare of the sea "coming for her", while the narrator of Reeves' poem depicts the sea spraying water "over the cliffs", which it could only do if there were large waves. However, Reeves' narrator also describes the sea on a calm day when it is "quiet", and so presents a more balanced image of the sea to the reader. This reflects how 'At Sea' shows an individual's thoughts and feelings while 'The Sea' explores the nature of the sea itself.

- The two poets use language differently in their poems. Reeves uses adjectives such as "Giant and grey" and onomatopoeia such as "howls" to describe the sea. These techniques help the reader to vividly imagine what the sea looks and sounds like. Copley, on the other hand, gives minimal description of the sea itself. She gives the most detail at the end of the poem, when the woman feels the "high tide's breakers' / chill in her arms" at the end of the poem. The lack of detail until this point makes the sea seem mysterious and ominous. It also makes the image of the woman with the waves in her arms even more shocking, because it suggests she has been suddenly overcome by the sea.

- Both poems personify the sea, but in different ways. Copley describes the sea as "coming for" the woman in the poem and "creeping in" through the door. This portrays the sea as an intruder to emphasise the woman's negative feelings towards it. Reeves, however, personifies the sea as a dog to show that it can behave differently at different times (e.g. calm or rough), which is reflected in the varying behaviour of a dog. In both cases, using personification allows the poet to clearly express the particular qualities of the sea that they want to highlight to the reader.

- Both poems use an irregular rhythm and varying line lengths. In 'At Sea' this creates an unsettled tone, reflecting the erratic nature of the woman's thoughts and feelings. In the first two stanzas of 'The Sea', it shows the turbulent nature of the sea. However, where 'At Sea' does not use rhyme, 'The Sea' includes rhyme both at the end of lines and within lines, such as "The rumbling, tumbling stones". The use of rhyme helps to create a clear sense of the sea's movement back and forth for the reader and emphasises its ceaselessness.

- Both poems are structured to describe the sea at different times. However, 'The Sea' covers a much longer period of time — more than one season — to give an overview of the sea's behaviour over time. 'At Sea', on the other hand, focuses intently on just a day, a night and the next day. This focus helps the reader to get to know the woman and her struggles through a specific period of time and understand her sense of monotony and fear of the sea more deeply.

Page 17 — Horse Whisperer

Q1 The poem is about a horse whisperer who tames unruly horses, but is driven away after the introduction of machinery. They get revenge on those who drove them out by placing curses on their prized horses.

Q2 "They" refers to horse owners, most likely farmers, who needed the horse whisperer to tame their disturbed horses.

Q3 Repeating the line at the beginning of two stanzas shows that the narrator was often asked by the farmers to help them, showing how valuable the narrator was. However, the fact they "shouted" for the narrator suggests the farmers didn't fully respect them.

Q4 "so I could lead the horses, / like helpless children, to safety" is an example of a simile. By comparing the horses to children, the narrator is presented as a protective parental figure, who is compassionate and able to control the horses.

Q5 The third stanza marks a turning point in the poem as the narrator begins to lose control — caesurae are introduced, sentences become shorter, and the language becomes less figurative. These techniques reflect the narrator's turmoil and how their life is disrupted by the arrival of modern machinery.

Q6 a) "a charm to draw the tender giants / to my hands" creates a positive atmosphere, as the charm seems to give the narrator the power to bring horses under their control.

b) "A foul hex above a stable door / so a trusted stallion could be ridden / no more" creates a negative atmosphere, as the words "foul hex" sound sinister and menacing. This is heightened through the internal rhyme of "door" and "no more", which has a chant-like quality, as though it is an evil spell.

Q7 The poet uses the simile of the tractor coming "over the fields /

Answers

like a warning" to create a sense of foreboding and to present the narrator's dislike of machinery. This idea is reinforced when the narrator states "I was the life-blood no longer", as it suggests that they have been replaced by machines.

Q8 The enjambment literally breaks up the phrase and isolates "no more". This emphasises the suddenness of the horse's inability to be ridden.

Q9 The narrator assigns animalistic qualities to themselves and joins the other outcast horse whisperers in fleeing the country. The word "stampede" suggests that they stayed close together for protection and that they fled very quickly and uncontrollably — in the same way the horses they used to tame might have.

Q10 a) The first four stanzas of the poem use the past tense, while the final stanza changes to the present tense with the sentence "Still I miss them."

b) Past tense is used to describe the narrator's memories of being a horse whisperer, which creates a sense of nostalgia and helps to convey the idea that a way of life has been lost. The use of the present tense in the final stanza helps to create sympathy for the narrator, by showing that their sense of loss hasn't diminished over time.

Q11 Although the narrator is originally presented as being in control of themselves and the horses, they slowly begin to lose this as the poem progresses. This is emphasised by the way the stanzas and line lengths gradually become shorter. After they lose their place in society, they enact revenge on those who drove them out, suggesting they attempt to regain some form of control.

Page 19 — The Bereavement of the Lion-Keeper

Q1 The poem is about an old zookeeper who stays on to look after a lion in the zoo after it has closed.

Q2 The keeper stayed "long after his pay stopped," suggesting that the zoo had closed, and he stayed on out of love for the lion. Even though he was hungry himself ("times grew hungrier"), the keeper still begged for food for the lion, not for himself.

Q3 Describing how "bombs fell" suggests that the zoo is in some kind of war zone. However, even with bombs falling, the keeper and the lion still felt safe because they were together. This is emphasised by the soothing words "wrapped" and "warmth", which contrast with the fear implied by the falling bombs and suggest a comforting physical bond.

Q4 The poet uses sound ("deepest purr in the world"), touch ("plunge fingers"), smell ("pungent scent") and sight ("rough glowing fur") to create a strong sense of what the lion was like. The descriptions give the impression of a gentle, loving and mutual relationship, even though man is expected to be afraid of lions and lions are predators.

Q5 a) Both the lion and the keeper are "moth-eaten" and "growing old together". The narrator states that "times grew hungrier", which suggests that food was scarce and both the keeper and the lion were at risk of starvation.

b) It makes the reader pity the old man, who was living in poverty and struggling to survive. It also suggests that, after the lion dies, the old man probably won't have long to live.

Q6 The keeper's love and devotion to the lion are presented in the first four stanzas, such as in the phrase "curled close", which shows how he takes comfort in being near the lion. The final two stanzas show the keeper's sense of loss after the lion dies — because he "knows no way to let go", he cannot move on and seems helpless.

Q7 You are left with a feeling that the old man doesn't have much to look forward to, as he struggles to move on and adjust to being merely "an old man in a city" — it is as though he has no identity without the lion. Also, the idea that "elderly lions / were not immortal" hints that humans aren't either. But there is hope in the idea that humans can be kind, caring, loving and loyal.

Q8 The stanzas beginning with "Who" reflect the keeper's certainty about his life, and the rhythm of his daily routine. The final stanza starts with a lower case "but". It also uses enjambment and marks the change of subject to how the keeper is struggling to accept the lion's death and "knows no way to let go". This emphasises the impact of the lion's death on the lion keeper, showing how the bereavement has destroyed the rhythm of his daily life.

Q9 The final stanza powerfully conveys how lost the keeper feels without the lion, that he knew "no way to let go / of love"; his love of the lion is compared to "sunlight", and when the lion dies he is in the dark. The final short line "without a lion" emphasises his feeling of loss.

Exam-style Question

You'll need to spend about 45 minutes on this, and your answer will probably bring in some of the things you thought about when you answered the other questions on the two poems. These are some points you could mention:

- Both poems present a human as being close to animals. In Forster's poem, the narrator describes the horses as "tender giants". The use of the adjective "tender" suggests that, despite their large size, the narrator sees the horses as gentle creatures and has a caring relationship with them. Similarly, in Pugh's poem, the alliteration in "curled close" emphasises the keeper's closeness with the lion.

- Both poems show humans caring for animals. In 'Horse Whisperer', the narrator leads the horses "like helpless children, to safety". This simile suggests the narrator views the horses as innocent and vulnerable, and so feels responsible for them. In Pugh's poem, the keeper is similarly caring in that he cuts up meat for the lion as "his teeth were gone", characterising the keeper as warm-hearted. Both of these images present humans who are protective and parental towards animals.

- Both poems show a sense of appreciation for the animals they feature. In 'Horse Whisperer', the narrator describes the horses' "glistening veins". This description shows that the narrator associates them with light, which is often seen as a symbolic positive force, emphasising how much he admires them. The lion-keeper in Pugh's poem, meanwhile, gets comfort from the lion by curling up to him to sleep. The description of how he does this "as the bombs fell" suggests that lying next to the lion was reassuring for him. Humans are therefore shown to have very positive relationships with animals in both these poems.

- The narrator of 'Horse Whisperer' presents horses as powerful, as shown through the description of their "shimmering muscles", which suggests they have great physical strength. In contrast, the lion in Pugh's poem is presented as much weaker. It is described as "elderly" and "moth-eaten", which suggests that the lion is a shadow of its former self, making the reader feel pity for it. These differences suggest that the horse whisperer's relationship with the horses is based on admiration and awe, even though he cares for them, while the relationship between the lion and the lion-keeper is about mutual comfort.

- Both poems show people who are torn away from the animals they care for, albeit in different ways, and they suffer emotionally as a result. In 'Horse Whisperer', the horse whisperer is forced to flee, leaving the horses behind. The narrator's sense of loss after being torn away from the horses is emphasised by the short sentence "Still I miss them." This sentence conveys a clear, direct message to the reader, encouraging them to

Answers

recognise the significance of the narrator's loss. In contrast, in Pugh's poem, the lion-keeper was torn away from the lion by its death. His feeling of loss is shown by the idea of having to "walk out of sunlight", symbolically suggesting that he feels hopeless after the lion's death.

- In both poems, aspects of form and structure reflect the suffering of the people in them when their connection with the animals they care for is broken. In 'Horse Whisperer', the lines in the final stanza gradually become shorter. This emphasises the distance the narrator feels from the horses that they had to leave behind. In Pugh's poem, the final stanza breaks the pattern of the previous stanzas in that it starts with "but" rather than "Who". This highlights a big change in the keeper's life and emphasises how he knows "no way to let go" of his love for the lost lion, causing the reader to feel sympathy for the keeper.

Page 21 — Originally

Q1 The poem is about a child who remembers when she and her family emigrated to another country, and the difficulties they faced during and after moving.

Q2 The narrator is presented as scared through the use of the phrase "fell through the fields", which creates a dangerous mood and emphasises the narrator's lack of control. This is emphasised as she is "holding" the "paw" of a toy, showing she also needs emotional comfort.

Q3 The repetition is almost like a chant, which creates the sense that her brothers are desperate to go back home. The repetition covers two lines, which creates a visual distance between the two words and reflects the distance the boys feel from their home.

Q4 The transition from first-person plural to first-person singular reinforces the narrator's sense of isolation to the reader, as it suggests she has been forced to become more independent in her new home. It suggests she no longer feels so protected by her family and feels more alone and vulnerable due to moving away from her familiar home to a new and unknown place.

Q5 This metaphor compares growing up to moving away. It highlights how getting older is always a big change, that this change is universal in that everyone goes through it, and that the changes are constant throughout childhood.

Q6 The second stanza has a mix of long and short sentences, enjambment, end-stopping and caesurae. This creates an irregular rhythm that reflects the narrator's feeling of uncertainty and confusion.

Q7 Seeing the "big boys / eating worms" is presented as shocking and confusing for the narrator, as the image is seen in an "unimagined" area and the boys are "shouting words" she doesn't understand — seeing them eat worms is also strange and troubling. Later though, when she sees her brother "swallow a slug", she only feels a "skelf of shame". Her reaction has changed, and now she is more used to this sort of behaviour. This change in the narrator's attitude shows that she has become more integrated into her new culture.

Q8 This shows that although the narrator is starting to fit into her new country, she has retained her Scottish dialect. This emphasises how important her cultural identity is to her.

Q9 The simile "my tongue / shedding its skin like a snake" compares the narrator losing her accent to a snake shedding its skin. The sibilance mimics the sound of a snake hissing, emphasising the image and suggesting that the narrator's change is a natural (although arguably horrifying) process.

Q10 The use of direct speech, such as *Where do you come from?*, directly involves the reader, making them feel immersed in what the narrator feels as well as encouraging them to question their own roots and experiences.

Q11 The poem lacks a fixed rhyme scheme, which reflects the narrator's insecurities and lack of control in her unfamiliar new home. However, lines 22 and 23 contain the internal rhyme "space" and "place", which could suggest the narrator is getting used to her new home.

Q12 The narrator is unsure about her identity, as shown through the final word "hesitate". Along with the question *Originally?*, this suggests that the idea of which place she identifies with the most has been blurred and she may be considering that her new home now forms part of her identity.

Page 23 — Hard Water

Q1 The poem is about a narrator who remembers a holiday to Wales and how they experienced the soft water there. The poem then shifts to the narrator describing their hometown and appreciating both the hard water and the people.

Q2 The first-person narrator gives the reader a personal insight into hard water and the narrator's connection with it. It also emphasises the personal connection between the hard water and the narrator's local community.

Q3 The poem is written in free verse, which reflects the "straight talk" of the narrator's hometown. With its irregular metre, the form also

reflects the "not quite clean" characteristic of hard water.

Q4 The tone becomes simpler and more appreciative in the second stanza, which is shown in line 4: "but I loved coming home to this" The word "but" reflects the "straight talk" and introduces the matter-of-fact tone.

Q5 The monosyllabic, one-word sentences used to describe the hard water reflect the flat pronunciation and vowels of the local accent, and so create a connection between the water and the local people.

Q6 The poet uses an extended metaphor to compare the hard water to the narrator's hometown and its residents.

Q7 The phrase "sour steam" is an example of sibilance. The repeated 's' sound mirrors the hissing sound of the cooling towers, immersing the reader in the brewery town setting.

Q8 The "different cleverness" refers to the local, hardworking community. Although the narrator has had "book-learning", they believe that the "early mornings" of hard work are still a type of cleverness.

Q9 The narrator states that they "loved coming home" to the hard water to highlight their sense of pride in it. As the poem uses this hard water as an extended metaphor for their hometown, it can be seen that the narrator shares the same sense of pride for their hometown.

Q10 a) "don't get mardy"

b) The dialect is used in brief, colloquial examples of direct speech, giving the reader a better sense of what the local speech sounds like. By using dialect words, the blunt and straight-talking nature of the locals is emphasised, further reinforcing the poem's extended metaphor.

Exam-style Question

You'll need to spend about 45 minutes on this, and your answer will probably bring in some of the things you thought about when you answered the other questions on the two poems. These are some points you could mention:

- Both poems describe the feelings of their narrators about different places in which they have lived. However, the narrator of 'Originally' moves away from her roots, whereas the narrator of 'Hard Water' has returned to their roots. Duffy's narrator describes how "the miles rushed back to the city", which personifies "miles" and uses the onomatopoeic verb "rushed" to create the sense that she is moving away from her roots quickly. The narrator of 'Hard Water' is presented as "coming home", which suggests a warm and close connection to their roots.

Answers

- Both narrators express a fondness for their roots. In 'Originally', the narrator states "*I want our own country*", which uses the possessive word "*our*" to imply to the reader that the narrator feels a sense of ownership over it. In 'Hard Water', the narrator "loved coming home" despite briefly trying the "soft stuff" in Wales. This shows how they are glad to be coming back to their hometown and its hard water.

- Both narrators have to adjust to the places that they describe. In 'Originally', the narrator recalls changing after moving to a new place. The simile "my tongue / shedding its skin like a snake" suggests she easily lost her old way of speaking, as snakes shed skin naturally. This implies that, despite the narrator's early negative feelings, she easily adjusted to her new way of speaking. In contrast, in 'Hard Water', the narrator describes the water's "little fizz of anxiety", which could be a metaphor for the narrator's anxious feelings when coming home. However, the more gentle word "settle" juxtaposes this, giving the reader the impression that the narrator has adjusted to being in their hometown again.

- Both narrators show a fondness for their linguistic roots, which are connected to the places that they describe. In Duffy's poem, the phrase a "skelf of shame" shows how the narrator has retained her Scottish dialect in her new country, suggesting it's an integral part of her identity. However, her tongue sheds "its skin like a snake", implying that her identity is undergoing change. In 'Hard Water', the narrator describes the "straight talk", showing an appreciation of the local accent, particularly how "Flat" and "Straight" it is. The narrator uses direct speech such as "*don't get mardy*" to give the reader a better understanding of what the dialect sounds like.

- The narrator of 'Originally' is presented as feeling like she doesn't belong in a place, whereas the narrator of 'Hard Water' feels accepted in their hometown. In Duffy's poem, the narrator's feelings about a place are revealed to the reader through the use of a question in "*Originally? And I hesitate.*" This hesitation suggests the narrator is uncertain about which place she identifies with most — her former home or her new one. In contrast, the narrator of 'Hard Water' seems to feel at home in the place they grew up, stating they feel marked as "belonging, regardless". These references are both from the final lines of each poem, which shows the significance of ideas of belonging and acceptance in both poems.

- Both poems are written in free verse, which reflects each narrator's feelings

towards a place. The lack of a rhyme scheme in 'Originally' creates a sense of irregularity, which highlights the narrator's insecurities. However, the internal rhyme of "space" and "place" in lines 22-23 hint that the narrator is becoming less insecure. 'Hard Water' is also written in free verse. This reflects the "straight talk" and therefore emphasises how the narrator appreciates the "blunt" local dialect. The free verse form in 'Originally' suggests unfamiliarity and uncertainty, whereas in 'Hard Water' it hints at an attachment to the locals.

Page 25 — Tattoos

Q1   The poem is about someone who remembers looking at their grandmother's tattoos and how they faded as she aged.

Q2   The grandchild's point of view creates a more objective description of the tattoos and how they changed. It also allows a shift from childlike descriptions of the tattoos to more abstract and mature ones.

Q3   Admiration for the narrator's grandmother is shown through the colourful and lively imagery used when remembering her tattoos. However, the narrator is more sorrowful in the last 7 lines as they remember her losing her memory and dying. This is reflected by the steady rhythm, which creates a solemn mood.

Q4   The tattoos represent the grandmother's ageing process — as she aged, the once bright and colourful tattoos of her youth faded to reflect how her body and mind deteriorated.

Q5   The poet may have used language associated with sailing to reflect the grandmother's life. Initially, the galleon represents a sense of adventure, and is strong and sturdy, reflecting the boldness of the grandmother's youth. However, it later comes "to rest", emphasising the certainty of ageing and death.

Q6   The word "bravado" suggests the grandmother lived a confident, carefree life in her youth — perhaps to the point of overconfidence.

Q7   The narrator found their grandmother fascinating when they were a young child, as shown through the phrase "mysterious as runes". This relates the grandmother's tattoos to magical letters of ancient alphabets, suggesting the narrator found her to be mysterious. Now the narrator is older, the descriptions are more grave to reflect their sadness at their grandmother ageing.

Q8   The poem consists of one continuous stanza that reflects the grandmother's life. The irregularity of the first half of the poem represents her

adventurous, varied youth. Then, after line 17, the shorter lines symbolise her life fading away over time in the same way her tattoos faded.

Q9   The image of her world shrinking "to a small island in the brain" suggests that the grandmother's mental capability has deteriorated, and that she can only think about 'small' things now, rather than thinking deeply. It may also reflect the fact that her life could have become smaller, perhaps due to not being able to leave the house so easily and not being able to be as adventurous as she used to be.

Q10   The metaphor of her memory as shipwrecked implies that her memory was destroyed, as though she suffered from a disease. It also suggests this deterioration was violent and catastrophic.

Q11   The use of the maritime measurement "fathom" further reinforces the theme of discovery and sailing. One fathom is equal to six feet, so the poet could be implying that the grandmother has died and been buried 'six feet under'.

Page 27 — The Ageing Schoolmaster

Q1   In the poem, a schoolmaster is thinking about how he will eventually die. He fondly remembers his youth and has no desire to upset his young pupils by telling them they will die.

Q2   Autumn "finds" the narrator, which suggests that the narrator has a passive role compared to the passing of time, which controls him. The narrator almost seems to be accepting of this.

Q3   The second stanza has a resigned mood. This is created as the narrator knows "absolutely" that he will not "reacquaint" himself with "joy". However, a nostalgic mood is also created when the narrator thinks of when he "rolled, a gormless boy", as it suggests he had fun in his youth.

Q4   While the use of words such as "rollicked" presents the narrator's childhood as carefree, he also states that he feels "no pinch or prick of envy" when he sees his younger pupils. This implies that although he enjoyed his childhood, he doesn't long to return to it.

Q5   The phrase "I sniff the smell of ink and chalk and my mortality" appeals to the sense of smell. It shows how mortality has pervaded the classroom, suggesting the narrator strongly links the two and that mortality is ever present in his mind.

Q6   He could either be referring to the classroom or to the narrator's life as an older adult, as "chill"

Answers

and "autumnal" are associated with the later half of the year.

Q7 The image of the "april faces / That gleam" before the narrator "like apples ranged on shelves" is a simile. It compares the pupils to shiny apples. The way they "gleam" presents them as keen and optimistic in contrast to the narrator. The fact that the pupils are compared to fresh fruit emphasises the idea that they are young and much further away from death than the narrator.

Q8 a) The poet presents both the narrator in his youth and the young pupils as being optimistic and blissfully unaware of their own mortality.

b) Getting older is presented as a process that is out of the narrator's control. He wonders "when precisely tolled the bell" that brought him into adulthood and was "summoned" from his childhood, which suggests that time has control over him.

c) The poet presents death as a "huge inevitability", meaning it is a certainty that weighs down heavily on the narrator. Because death preoccupies the thoughts of the only adult in the poem, the poet could be implying that death only becomes an issue when you age and lose your sense of youthful naivety.

Q9 The poet uses the seasons of summer and autumn to reflect parts of the human life span. The "summer liberties" are presented as being the points in life when you are happiest and freest, as shown when the narrator "rollicked round the playground". Autumn is symbolic of the narrator's adult years — autumn is the season where plants begin to die, which reflects the narrator growing older.

Q10 The image of "death, who carries off all the prizes" is an example of personification. It presents death as a victor in a competition, which makes death seem more real and present to the reader.

Exam-style Question

You'll need to spend about 45 minutes on this, and your answer will probably bring in some of the things you thought about when you answered the other questions on the two poems. These are some points you could mention:

- 'Tattoos' presents the life of a grandmother through her tattoos and how they faded as she aged. The narrator is her grandchild, witnessing the ageing of their grandmother and describing how they "studied" her when growing up. In contrast, Scannell's poem is from the perspective of a schoolmaster who is himself ageing and who is now reflecting on his life from when he was

a "gormless boy". The perspective of a grandchild makes Patten's poem more poignant, because it shows the narrator's sadness for their grandmother. In 'The Ageing Schoolmaster', in contrast, there is a sense of fear as the narrator thinks of "the huge inevitability of death".

- Both poems compare the aged person at different points in their life. In 'Tattoos', the narrator imagines their grandmother "in her youth" before recounting how her "memory was shipwrecked". Similarly, in 'The Ageing Schoolmaster', the narrator remembers how he "rolled, a gormless boy". In doing this, each figure's ageing is emphasised to the reader through the contrast with their younger self.

- Both poems use sensory language to convey attitudes towards getting older. The narrator of Patten's poem focuses heavily on the sense of sight. They remember the "unblurred" tattoos and the bold "colours", but also how the tattoos faded. This helps the reader to visualise the effects of ageing on the grandmother. In 'The Ageing Schoolmaster', the narrator uses multiple senses, such as smell ("sniff"), touch ("prick") and sound ("tolled"), which suggests the notion of death not only plagues his thoughts, but has taken over his senses too.

- Both narrators use alliteration when describing the effects of ageing. In 'Tattoos', the narrator describes how no "burst blood vessels sullied / the breast of the blue-bird" in the grandmother's youth. The repeated 'b' sound almost recreates the sound of the vessels bursting, emphasising the grandmother's physical deterioration as she aged. In 'The Ageing Schoolmaster', the narrator describes how he "rolled" and "rollicked round the playground" when he was a child. This phrase uses alliteration of the 'r' sound to create a lively, upbeat rhythm, which gives the reader a strong sense that his youth was jovial and carefree.

- Imagery is used in both poems to emphasise the theme of ageing. The "needle-sharp" rose described in the first half of the poem could be a metaphor for the grandmother's intelligence and wit in her youth. However, in the final line, the rose has "gone to seed", which suggests the flower has faded. This represents how the grandmother lost her memory and therefore her intellectual ability in the years before she died. Similarly, in 'The Ageing Schoolmaster', the narrator describes how his pupils "gleam" before him "like apples ranged on shelves". This simile portrays the pupils as fresh and bright, like newly picked apples, emphasising their youthfulness and reinforcing how distanced the narrator feels from them.

- Both poets use form and structure in a way that reflects their ideas on life and ageing. Patten's poem is written in free verse with no set rhythm or rhyme scheme, reflecting the grandmother's adventurous personality as a younger person. However, it does include a turning point at line 15, at which point the poem focuses on the effects of ageing, presenting to the reader a clear contrast between the grandmother in her youth and in her older age. In contrast, Scannell's poem has a much more regular rhythm and rhyme scheme and is set out in five 4-line stanzas. This forces the reader to move through the poem in a more stately manner and reflects the narrator's academic background as well as his steady, resigned contemplation of ageing and mortality.

Page 29 — Island Man

Q1 The poem is about a man waking up after dreaming of his previous home on a Caribbean island, before gradually coming back to the reality of his life in London.

Q2 The line is very short, which makes the start of the poem abrupt, as if the man has woken up suddenly. It also helps to set the scene of the poem, giving the reader a sense of the time of day.

Q3 Referring to the man in the poem as "island man" emphasises his close connection to where he came from. It also suggests he feels separated from London, by emphasising that he is from a different place. Referring to him as an "island" might also make him seem emotionally cut-off to the reader, suggesting he may be lonely.

Q4 The lines show how important the sights and sounds of the Caribbean are to him, as they are in his thoughts and dreams at the point where he is starting to wake up. The fact that they are in his mind suggests a feeling of longing for his Caribbean island.

Q5 The repetition of the words creates a sense of confusion which might reflect the man's sleepiness as he wakes up. It also echoes the rocking sound of the tides that the man remembers on the island, helping the reader to imagine the experience of being on the island.

Q6 Words like "roar" and "surge" are used to describe the London traffic that the man can hear while he wakes. These words could also be used to describe the movement of the tide, suggesting that the man is imagining that he is actually near the Caribbean sea. The use of this language shows both that the man is disoriented or still dreaming, and also how strong his memories of the Caribbean are, as they influence the way he experiences London.

Answers

Q7 The phrase "fishermen pushing out to sea / the sun surfacing defiantly" uses sibilance. The soft 's' and 'sh' sounds echo the sounds of the sea, helping the reader to imagine being on the man's island. The sibilance also has a soothing effect, suggesting how much calmer and more relaxing the island was compared to London.

Q8 a) Bright colours are used in the description of the man's Caribbean island ("blue surf" and "emerald island"), while the only colour used to describe London is "grey".

b) The use of contrasting colours to describe the island and London makes the man's previous home seem like a beautiful paradise, while London seems dreary and drab.

Q9 Enjambment makes the poem seem disordered rather than carefully controlled. This reflects the man's sleepiness as he is waking up, showing that he is disoriented and isn't fully aware of his surroundings yet.

Q10 The increased spacing before "groggily groggily" emphasises these words to the reader, and therefore how disorientated the man feels as he begins to wake up. The way the phrase "to surge of wheels" is set far off to the right of the line also draws attention to this phrase and reflects how the jarring sounds of traffic are interrupting the man's dreams, just as the layout here interrupts the flow of the poem.

Q11 The final line, "Another London day", suggests that the man wakes up this way every morning and makes his life in London seem repetitive and boring. The line is separated from the rest of the poem, which reflects the fact that he has come out of his dream and must now face the reality of his day.

Page 31 — Remember

Q1 The poem is about the importance of remembering where we come from and the world around us — it describes several things the reader should "Remember", including their links to family and nature.

Q2 The phrase "Remember the sky that you were born under" encourages the reader to remember the place where they were born, while "know each of the star's stories" suggests they should be aware of their place in the universe. Both images emphasise to the reader the importance of nature in understanding the world.

Q3 Using the second person allows the narrator to develop a closer connection with the reader and encourages them to actively think about the ideas in the poem and how they relate to their own life.

Q4 Presenting the poem as one continuous stanza makes the different ideas in the poem flow into one another — this shows how all of the things to remember from "Remember the sky that you were born under" to "Remember the dance language is, that life is" are of equal importance to the narrator.

Q5 Enjambment is used in the sentence "Talk to them, / listen to them." This places emphasis on the word "listen", showing how important the narrator thinks learning about and being aware of your surroundings and nature is.

Q6 The sentence emphasises the importance of family and ancestry in understanding how we come to be who we are. The repetition of "her/hers" encourages the reader to think about the continuous line of women who have contributed to their life.

Q7 The poet personifies the wind by saying "Remember the wind. Remember her voice. She knows the / origin of this universe." The wind is described as having a voice and a deep understanding of the universe. This stresses how important the narrator believes nature is, as it helps people to feel more connected to the universe as a whole.

Q8 Repeating the imperative "Remember" as a command throughout the poem puts across a sense of urgency to the reader about not forgetting their place in the world. The repetition also mimics the action of remembering itself, and so emphasises to the reader the importance of constantly remembering and being aware of the world around them.

Q9 A metaphor is used in the phrase "you are all people and all people / are you." This stresses how every individual is connected to everyone else. Describing this idea in two different ways, moving from "you" to "all people" and then back to "you", emphasises this message by reinforcing the link between the reader and the rest of society.

Q10 The overall mood of the poem is thoughtful and contemplative. This is created by the continuous appeals to the reader to "Remember", which suggest that the reader should pause and take the time to really think about the world around them and their heritage. The frequent references to nature also help to create a calm tone in the poem.

Exam-style Question

You'll need to spend about 45 minutes on this, and your answer will probably bring in some of the things you thought about when you answered the other questions on the two poems. These are some points you could mention:

- 'Island Man' explores memory by focusing on the way a man from the Caribbean, now living in London, is reminded of his former home by the traffic sounds of urban London. Rather than focusing on the memory of a specific place, 'Remember' is about memory more generally, with the narrator encouraging the reader to be aware of their place in the world and remember where they came from.

- Both poems use language related to place and landscape to emphasise the links between memory and personal identity. 'Island Man' refers to "his small emerald island" which the man returns to in his mind. The use of the possessive "his" shows the sense of belonging he feels towards the island — even though he is now in London, he still feels a close personal connection to the place. This shows how important the memory of the island is to him. Similarly, the narrator of 'Remember' says "Remember the earth whose skin you are". This metaphor shows the close relationship between a person's identity and their environment. It emphasises how important remembering nature is, because humans are a part of nature.

- Both poets use repetition to explore memory, but in different ways. 'Island Man' uses repetition to convey the effects of memory. In the poem, the words "comes back" are repeated as the man wakes up to the reality of his life in London. The repetition suggests returning to his normal life from his memory is a struggle, showing the powerful effect of his memories on him. 'Remember' uses repetition to emphasise the poet's main message. Anaphora is used to repeat the word "Remember" throughout the poem. This insistently emphasises to the reader the importance of considering their heritage and their place in the world, and consciously remembering these things.

- 'Island Man' presents a personal memory by using the third person to describe the experience of one individual. The description of the man as "island man" emphasises how the poem is about this one person and his memories of his original home. 'Remember', on the other hand, presents memory as more universal and part of a broader cultural heritage. The main way this is achieved is through the use of second-person address in sentences like "Remember you are this universe and this / universe is you." By addressing the reader in general, the poet emphasises how certain kinds of memory are shared by everyone, and encourages the reader to remember their links to all people and to all of nature.

Answers

- Both poems make use of rhyme and rhythm to present ideas about memory. 'Island Man' has no rhyme scheme, fixed rhythm or stanza length, and uses frequent enjambment, which all help to create a sense of the dreaminess and incoherence experienced by the man as he wakes up "groggily" and remembers where he really is. This suggests that the man's memories are overpowering for him. 'Remember' features a similar lack of rhyme scheme and several long, enjambed lines, which create a sense of flow in the poem. This suggests that remembering the things in the poem — your culture and your place in the world — should be natural and easy.

- Both poems use their final lines to emphasise their different perspectives on memory. The last line of 'Island Man' is "Another London day". The word "Another" conveys a sense of repetitiveness which suggests that the man's life in London is repetitive or boring. The reader is therefore left with the sense that the man wants to return to his memory of the island. The final line of 'Remember' is the single word "Remember." This acts as a final instruction to the reader to remember and be aware of everything the narrator has listed in the poem. Although the word is often repeated in the poem, here the narrator does not tell the reader to remember anything specific — the importance is placed on remembering itself, emphasising to the reader how important this is.

Section Three — Marking Sample Answers

Pages 36-37 — Listen Mr Oxford Don and Neighbours

Sample Answer Extract 1

a) 8-9

b) Two from, e.g.:
- It convincingly compares the way the poets use structure for the same purpose — to challenge prejudice.
- It is well supported with precise examples from both poems.
- It uses a variety of technical terms effectively.

Sample Answer Extract 2

a) 4-5

b) Two from, e.g.:
- It describes a clear similarity between the two poems.
- It should explore the effect that techniques have on the reader.
- It needs to use more technical terms.

Sample Answer Extract 3

a) 4-5

b) Two from, e.g.:
- It makes valid comparisons between the two poems.
- It uses relevant examples from both poems and gives some explanation of them.
- The examples could be explored and analysed in more detail.
- It could be improved with more technical terms.

Sample Answer Extract 4

a) 6-7

b) Two from, e.g.:
- It makes a thoughtful comparison of the poets' use of imagery.
- It uses technical terms correctly.
- It needs some more analysis of specific language features.

Pages 40-41 — Introduction to Poetry and Volumes

Sample Answer Extract 1

a) 4-5

b) Two from, e.g.:
- It makes a valid comparison between the two poems.
- It uses relevant references from both poems, but the examples could be more precise.
- It should explore the effect that techniques have on the reader in greater detail.
- It needs to use more technical terms.

Sample Answer Extract 2

a) 8-9

b) Two from, e.g.:
- It gives a detailed evaluation of the form and structure of the two poems.
- It critically compares the similarities and differences between the two poems.
- It uses a variety of different technical terms accurately and effectively.

Sample Answer Extract 3

a) 8-9

b) Two from, e.g.:
- It evaluates the language used in both poems in extensive detail.
- It explores in detail how features of the poem affect the reader.
- It integrates precise examples from the text that support the points being made.

Sample Answer Extract 4

a) 6-7

b) Two from, e.g.:
- It makes a focused comparison between the language used in the two poems.

- It uses relevant examples to support the points being made.
- It needs to analyse specific language features in greater depth.

Pages 44-45 — Below the Green Corrie and The Moment

Sample Answer Extract 1

a) 6-7

b) Two from, e.g.:
- It gives some relevant examples and integrates them well.
- It shows a good understanding of the language used in both poems.
- It could be improved with more technical terms.

Sample Answer Extract 2

a) 6-7

b) Two from, e.g.:
- It makes good comparisons on the use of personification in both poems.
- It explains the effects of the poets' techniques on the reader.
- Some of the quotes are not integrated into the argument.

Sample Answer Extract 3

a) 8-9

b) Two from, e.g.:
- It gives an insightful evaluation of the poets' use of form and structure.
- It uses a range of well-chosen examples from the text to support its points.
- It uses a wide range of relevant technical terms.

Sample Answer Extract 4

a) 4-5

b) Two from, e.g.:
- It clearly compares how the poets present nature in the two poems.
- It refers to the effects on the reader of the poets' choices.
- Examples from and references to the text are included, but these could be more specific and better integrated into the answer.
- It needs to use more technical terms to support the points being made.

Section Four — Practice Exam Questions

Pages 46-47 — Those Winter Sundays and My Father on His Shield

Q1

- In 'Those Winter Sundays' and 'My Father on His Shield', the narrators both reflect on relationships with their fathers, although the overall focus is slightly different. In 'Those Winter Sundays', the narrator considers the sacrifices their father made and regrets not fully

Answers

appreciating him, giving the poem a guilty tone. 'My Father on His Shield', on the other hand, is focused on the narrator's happy memories with their father, and their sadness because they can't "bring" their father "back".

- The relationship between a father and his child in 'Those Winter Sundays' is emotionally distant, as the narrator speaks "indifferently to" their father. The preposition "to" further suggests emotional distance, as it implies a one-sided relationship where the father isn't listened to in return. In contrast, the relationship in 'My Father on His Shield' is shown to be loving, with affection expressed through literal closeness rather than communication. For example, although the father doesn't speak, he protectively wraps the "rope in his fist / around" the narrator's "chest", where the image of holding the rope to keep his child secure suggests a strong bond.

- Both poets use a combination of caesurae and end-stopping to highlight key ideas within their poems. In 'Those Winter Sundays', these techniques are used to separate the sentence "No one ever thanked him." from the rest of the stanza. The poet's decision to isolate this sentence in particular emphasises the lack of gratitude shown towards the father and the narrator's lasting regret that they never thanked him. Similarly, in the first stanza of 'My Father on His Shield', a combination of end-stopping and a caesura is used to emphasise the sentence "I can't bring my father back." This helps the reader to understand the significance of the narrator's sadness that they "can't" bring their father back.

- Both poets suggest their narrator's appreciation for their father by describing the father doing strenuous activity. In 'Those Winter Sundays', the narrator describes their father's "cracked hands that ached". This consonance of the 'k' sound mimics the splitting of the father's skin, emphasising the laborious nature of his work. This suggests the narrator feels a sense of appreciation for their father as they reflect on the difficult labour he undertook for their benefit, showing a positive element to their relationship. The narrator of 'My Father on His Shield' remembers their father's "fists, the iron he pounded, / five-pound hammer ringing steel", which uses forceful consonance and the onomatopoeic word "ringing" to convey a sense of the narrator's awe at their father's strength. This emphasises the narrator's close relationship with their father and how much they looked up to him as a child.

- Both poems use form to convey the narrators' feelings about their fathers. 'Those Winter Sundays' appears to be based on the sonnet form, which usually consists of 14 lines, has a strict rhyme scheme and rhythm, and is traditionally used to express love or appreciation for someone. However, the poet breaks the traditional conventions by having no rhyme scheme, an irregular metre, and not directly expressing love. This reflects the conflict between how the narrator used to feel about their father and how they feel now. 'My Father on His Shield', in contrast, is written entirely in free verse, has no fixed rhythm or rhyme scheme, and has uneven line lengths. This reflects how the narrator doesn't feel complete or settled without their father. It suggests that the father may have brought orderliness or routine to the child's upbringing.

- The childhood memories presented in 'Those Winter Sundays' are negative. For example, the narrator describes the "chronic angers of that house", suggesting that it was an unhappy and volatile environment. That the narrator fears these "angers" while responding to a "call" from their father implies that they are caused by or linked to a poor relationship between the pair. In contrast, in 'My Father on His Shield', the narrator's childhood is presented positively to the reader. The use of onomatopoeia such as "whishing" helps the reader imagine the narrator's happy memories with their father, which emphasises the narrator's sadness at his loss.

Pages 48-49 — Flowers and Don't Say I Said

Q2

- The narrators of the two poems feel differently about the end of their relationships. The narrator of 'Flowers' seems calm, conveying a positive view of their former partner, and a sense of wistful regret about the end of their relationship. The narrator of 'Don't Say I Said', on the other hand, seems angry and hurt, and presents the end of their relationship in a broadly negative way.

- 'Flowers' is structured so as to reveal at the end of the poem that the narrator looks back wistfully on their relationship. The change of tone is indicated in the final three lines with the word "Now" and the change in time to talk about the present. The description of the flowers that have "lasted all this while" in these lines shows that the narrator is appreciative of the person they're addressing, even though the relationship is over. In contrast, 'Don't Say I Said' uses structure to highlight how the narrator is trying to pretend they are not affected by the end of their relationship. The narrator repeats the refrain "Don't say I said to say it" at the end of each stanza. The phrase is light and playful on the surface, but the way it is repeated

makes the narrator seem desperate, suggesting they are actually unhappy with how their relationship ended.

- 'Flowers' uses enjambment to create a stilted, awkward rhythm, such as in the sentence "You thought / I might not want your flowers." The enjambment emphasises the ex-partner's uncertainty and creates a fragmented tone, which hints to the reader that the narrator feels incomplete now that the relationship is over. 'Don't Say I Said' also has a slightly awkward rhythm, created by the enjambment of lines such as "And add that every day it / Seems I am harder to resist." This makes it seem as if the narrator's desperation to come across well makes them awkward, showing that a relationship's end can make people act in ways which reflect badly on them.

- The two poems use language to present contrasting attitudes towards the former partner. In 'Flowers', the narrator's ex-partner is presented positively. The short, simple sentence "You did." stresses the ex-partner's thoughtfulness, while the repetition of "smile" in the final stanza shows that, even though the relationship has ended, the narrator still views it positively. In 'Don't Say I Said', on the other hand, the narrator refers to their ex-partner as "you-know-who". This colloquial phrase uses monosyllabic words to convey to the reader the narrator's sense of anger, suggesting that they are so upset with their former partner that they cannot bring themselves to say his name.

- In 'Flowers', there is a sense of connection between the narrator and their former partner, created by the use of the second person ("you") to refer to him, and phrases such as "minds like ours", which suggest that the pair still have things in common. In contrast, the narrator of 'Don't Say I Said' refers to their ex-partner in the third person ("him"), which creates a sense of distance between them. This suggests that, despite the narrator's belief that "He might ask" about them, the connection they once had has now been lost.

- The two poems are very different in rhythm and tone, reflecting the narrators' contrasting feelings about the end of their relationships. 'Flowers' uses gentle rhymes like "ours" / "flowers", which give the poem a calm, peaceful tone. This reflects the narrator's positive view of their ex-partner, but it also makes the narrator seem wistful, conveying their feelings of regret that the relationship has come to an end. Conversely, the end-stopped double rhymes in 'Don't Say I Said' give the poem a frustrated tone, which communicates to the reader the narrator's feelings of anger and irritation with the way their relationship ended.

Glossary

alliteration	Where words that are close together start with the same sound, e.g. "scarcely snores".
anaphora	Where a word or phrase is repeated at the start of sentences or lines.
caesura (plural caesurae)	A pause in a line of poetry. E.g. the full stop in "It couldn't lie. Fell thick".
colloquial language	Informal language that sounds like ordinary speech, e.g. "too bloody deep for me".
consonance	Repetition of a consonant sound in nearby words, e.g. "cracked hands that ached".
contrast	When two things are described in a way which emphasises how different they are. E.g. a poet might contrast two different people or two different voices.
dialect	A variation of a language spoken by people from a particular place or background. Dialects might include different words or sentence constructions, e.g. "So mek dem send".
direct address	When the narrator speaks directly to the reader or another character, e.g. "How will you feel?"
direct speech	The actual words that are said by someone.
double rhyme	When two syllables rhyme, rather than just one, e.g. "convey it" and "say it".
empathy	The ability to imagine and understand someone else's feelings or experiences.
end-stopping	Finishing a line of poetry with the end of a phrase or sentence, usually marked by punctuation.
enjambment	When a sentence or phrase runs over from one line or stanza to the next.
figurative language	Language that is used in a non-literal way to create an effect, e.g. personification.
first person	Writing from the perspective of the narrator, written using words like 'I', 'me', 'we' and 'our'.
form	The type of poem, e.g. a sonnet or ballad, and the overall way it is written, e.g. the rhyme scheme.
free verse	Poetry that doesn't rhyme and has no regular rhythm or line length.
iambic pentameter	Poetry with a metre of ten syllables — five of them stressed, and five unstressed. The stress falls on every second syllable, e.g. "And when she died I felt no grief at all".
iambic tetrameter	Like iambic pentameter but with a metre of eight syllables — four stressed and four unstressed. E.g. "or press an ear against its hive".
imagery	Language that creates a picture in your mind. It includes metaphors, similes and personification.
imperative	An order or direction, e.g. "Remember the wind."
internal rhyme	When two or more words rhyme, and at least one of the words isn't at the end of a line. The rhyming words can be in the same line or nearby lines. E.g. "The rumbling, tumbling stones".
juxtaposition	When a poet puts two ideas, events, characters or descriptions close to each other to encourage the reader to contrast them. E.g. the juxtaposition of "love" and "anguish" in 'Handbag'.
language	The choice of words used. Different kinds of language have different effects.
metaphor	A way of describing something by saying that it is something else, e.g. "The sea is a hungry dog". An extended metaphor is a metaphor that is carried on, e.g. the tattoos metaphor in 'Tattoos'.
metre	The arrangement of stressed and unstressed syllables to create rhythm in a line of poetry.
monosyllables	Words with only one syllable, e.g. "her world shrank".

Glossary

Glossary

mood	The feel or atmosphere of a poem, e.g. humorous, peaceful, fearful.
narrative	Writing that tells a story, e.g. 'Horse Whisperer'.
narrative viewpoint	The perspective that a text is written from, e.g. first-person point of view.
narrator	The person speaking the words. E.g. the narrator of 'Listen Mr Oxford Don' is an immigrant.
onomatopoeia	A word that sounds like the thing it's describing, e.g. "click" and "whistling" in 'Jumper'.
personification	Describing a non-living thing as if it's a person. E.g. "this rain had forgotten the sea".
phonetic spellings	When words are spelt as they sound rather than with their usual spelling, e.g. "dem" instead of "them". It's often used to show that someone is speaking with a certain accent or dialect.
refrain	A line or stanza in a poem that is repeated. E.g. "Don't say I said to say it" in 'Don't Say I Said'.
repetition	The technique of repeating words, phrases, ideas or images for effect.
rhyme scheme	A pattern of rhyming words in a poem. E.g. 'Flowers' has an ABCB rhyme scheme — this means that the second and fourth lines in each stanza rhyme.
rhyming triplet	Three rhyming lines that are next to each other.
rhythm	A pattern of sounds created by the arrangement of stressed and unstressed syllables.
second person	When the narrator talks directly to another person, written using words like "you".
sensory language	Language that appeals to any of the five senses. E.g. "I let a different cleverness wash my tongue."
sibilance	Repetition of 's' and 'sh' sounds, e.g. "she dusts the house, / sweeps".
simile	A way of describing something by comparing it to something else, usually by using the words "like" or "as". E.g. "the tractor came over the fields / like a warning".
sonnet	A form of poem with fourteen lines, that usually follows a clear rhyme scheme.
stanza	A group of lines in a poem.
structure	The order and arrangement of ideas in a poem, e.g. if the poem is split into stanzas.
syllable	A single unit of sound within a word. E.g. "all" has one syllable, "always" has two.
symbolism	When an object stands for something else. E.g. the tractor in 'Horse Whisperer' symbolises the arrival of modern machinery.
syntax	The arrangement of words in a sentence or phrase so that they make sense.
tense	Writing about the past, present or future. E.g. "I walked" is the past tense, "I walk" is the present tense and "I will walk" is the future tense.
theme	An idea or topic that's important in a poem. E.g. a poem could be based on the theme of love.
third person	When a poet writes about someone who isn't the speaker, written using words like "he" or "she".
tone	The mood or feelings suggested by the way the narrator writes, e.g. bitter, reflective.
voice	The characteristics of the person narrating the poem. Poems are usually written either using the poet's voice, as if they're speaking to you directly, or the voice of a character.

Acknowledgements

We would like to thank the following copyright holders:

Cover quote: LISTEN, MR OXFORD DON copyright © 1985 by John Agard reproduced by kind permission of John Agard c/o Caroline Sheldon Literary Agency Ltd.

'Ninetieth Birthday' from COLLECTED POEMS 1945-1990 by RS Thomas. Published by The Orion Publishing Group. © 1993 R. S. Thomas.

'My Grandmother' by Elizabeth Jennings from The Collected Poems, Carcanet Press.

'Handbag' by Ruth Fainlight from 'New and Collected Poems', Bloodaxe Books, 2010.

'Jumper' by Tony Harrison published by Faber & Faber Ltd.

'At Sea' by Jennifer Copley, first published in 2003 by Arrowhead Press.

'The Sea' by James Reeves from Complete Poems for Children, Faber & Faber.

'Horse Whisperer' by Andrew Forster from Fear of Thunder (Flambard Press).

'The Bereavement of the Lion-Keeper' from Sheenagh Pugh: The Movement of Bodies (Seren, 2005).

'Originally' from The Other Country by Carol Ann Duffy. Published by Anvil Press Poetry, 1990. Copyright © Carol Ann Duffy. Reproduced by permission of the author c/o Rogers, Coleridge & White Ltd., 20 Powis Mews, London W11 1JN.

From Hard Water by Jean Sprackland. Published by Jonathan Cape. Reprinted by permission of The Random House Group Limited. © 2003.

'Tattoos' from Selected Poems by Brian Patten. Published by Penguin, 2005. Copyright © Brian Patten. Reproduced by permission of the author c/o Rogers, Coleridge & White Ltd., 20 Powis Mews, London W11 1JN.

'Ageing Schoolmaster' by Vernon Scannell from Collected Poems 1950-1993 (Faber).

The Fat Black Woman's Poems Copyright © Grace Nichols 1984. Reproduced with permission of Curtis Brown Ltd, London on behalf of Grace Nichols.

'Remember'. Copyright © 1983 by Joy Harjo, from SHE HAD SOME HORSES by Joy Harjo. Used by permission of W. W. Norton & Company, Inc.

LISTEN, MR OXFORD DON copyright © 1985 by John Agard reproduced by kind permission of John Agard c/o Caroline Sheldon Literary Agency Ltd.

'Neighbours' by Benjamin Zephaniah from Propa Propaganda (Bloodaxe Books, 1996). Reproduced with permission of Bloodaxe Books. www.bloodaxebooks.com.

Billy Collins, 'Introduction to Poetry' from The Apple That Astonished Paris. Copyright © 1988, 1996 by Billy Collins. Reprinted with the permission of The Permissions Company, Inc., on behalf of the University of Arkansas Press, www.uapress.com.

'Volumes' by Jo Shapcott from 'Her Book', published by Faber & Faber Ltd.

'Below the Green Corrie' by Norman MacCaig from Poems of Norman MacCaig published by Birlinn Limited. Reproduced with permission of the Licensor through PLSclear.

'The Moment' by Margaret Atwood. Reproduced with permission of Curtis Brown Group Ltd, on behalf of O. W. Toad Ltd. Copyright © O W Toad, 1995.

'Those Winter Sundays'. Copyright © 1966 by Robert Hayden, from COLLECTED POEMS OF ROBERT HAYDEN by Robert Hayden, edited by Frederick Glaysher. Used by permission of Liveright Publishing Corporation.

Walt MacDonald's poem, 'My Father on His Shield', is from the collection, Blessings the Body Gave (1998), and is reprinted with permission from the Ohio State University Press.

'Flowers' by Wendy Cope from 'Two Cures for Love', published by Faber & Faber Ltd.

'Don't Say I Said' from Pessimism for Beginners by Sophie Hannah (Carcanet Press Limited, 2007).

Every effort has been made to locate copyright holders and obtain permission to reproduce sources. For those sources where it has been difficult to trace the copyright holder of the work, we would be grateful for information. If any copyright holder would like us to make an amendment to the acknowledgements, please notify us and we will gladly update the book at the next reprint. Thank you.